PLAYS WITHOUT THEATRES

Recollections of
The Compass Players
Travelling Theatre 1944 - 1952

compiled and edited by Pamela Dellar

Foreword by Neil Sissons

Highgate Publications (Beverley) Ltd
1989

Published by Highgate Publications (Beverley) Ltd.
24 Wylies Road, Beverley, HU17 7AP
Telephone (0482) 866826

Printed and Typeset in 10 on 11 Plantin by
B.A. Press, 2-4 Newbegin, Lairgate, Beverley, HU17 8EG
Telephone (04482) 882232

British Library Cataloguing in Publication Data

Plays without theatres.
   1. Great Britain. Theatre. Touring companies. Compass Players, history
   I. Dellar, Pamela, 1927-
   792'.0941

ISBN 0-948929-27-8

FOREWORD

by Neil Sissons
Artistic Director, Compass Theatre Company,
the New Ensemble, Sheffield

I was delighted to be asked to provide a foreword for **Plays Without Theatres** for it seems that the experiences and problems encountered by The Compass Players of the 1940s have a very familiar feel to the ones encountered by us in the 1980s.

We too have enjoyed a love/hate relationship with our various means of transport: vans with an uncanny knack of breaking down in the middle of torrentially rainy nights, vans that make remarkable recoveries at the first sight of the breakdown man's car headlights, and vans whose interiors can, after long bouts of touring, seem more familiar than home.

Like the Compass before us, we too play the classics, touring, with little subsidy, throughout Great Britain and playing Shakespeare in any space that wants us. We even seem to play the same kind of venues, from village halls and working men's clubs to large theatres, playing anything from one night stands to full weeks, bringing theatre to places often remote and unserved by other companies.

It is exciting to feel that we exist in the long tradition of travelling players. I am sure that the book will be a fascinating and revealing read for anyone interested in theatre and the life of touring theatre companies.

INTRODUCTION

The Compass Players was founded in 1944 by John Crockett. From their base in a large house in Gloucestershire they travelled the length and breadth of England, Scotland and Wales. When they were touring in the North East they were also based at Ormesby Hall near Middlesbrough. The aim of the company was to take plays of quality to those parts of the country where there was no live theatre. Like many companies today, but not then, they worked as a co-operative, sharing everything and doing anything from stage management and prop making to acting.

John Crockett wrote to me in 1986 when he knew that he had only a few months to live, and asked me to write about The Compass Players. At first I was hesitant — until I found that everyone whom I invited to contribute wanted to join me in telling the story because, like me, they felt those years had been exceptional in their lives. The result is this book which, nearly half a century later, gives an insight into the ideals and way of life of a small group of travelling players in wartime and immediate post-war Britain.

The book has fallen into two parts. The first part describes how the company began and the experiences of those who pioneered the work. In the second part former members of the company, now with a lifetime of working in drama and theatre, tell of that special period in their career.

It has been very much a Compass-style production. I have collected and edited the contributions: John Ringham word processed and made constructive comments; Collin Hansen compiled the index; Armine Sandford gave much valuable advice and, with Maurice Daniels, helped to select the photographs; Anne Crockett rang round to encourage people to finish their contributions; Mary and Elizabeth Crockett designed the cover from John Crockett's original illustration for an earlier children's book; and everyone agreed to help with distribution and gave encouragement when the task seemed to be getting impossible.

My grateful thanks go to Janet Blackman of Hull University for her advice and encouragement and to Sue Wilsea who helped in the very early and insecure stages. Also to 'Rob' Robinson, Armine's husband, who spent several holidays listening to discussions and unedited contributions. Thanks are also due to John Markham of Highgate Publications (Beverley), Joan Burns who helped to launch the book in Gloucestershire and to Anne Sweeney who typed for us and assures us that she enjoyed it.

For permission to print copyright material we gratefully acknowledge the following: Wilfred Harrison and executors of the estate of R.H. Ward for permission to print an unpublished letter; Molly Sole for permission to print her contribution; Oxford University Press for permission to reprint an extract from the memoirs of Charles Brasch; and Anne Crockett for permission to print a selection of paintings and photographs by John Crockett.

PAMELA DELLAR, 1989

CONTENTS

PART ONE

Early Days and New Plays 1944 - 48

Commentary by Pamela Dellar with contributions from —   Leslie Hardie
Brian Stapleton
Paula Burton
Anne Crockett

PART TWO

1948 - 1952

'And now begins a new circle, the ring
Of another generation, and another
Revolution of the wheeling heavens; light
To light is added and the starry forges glow
In confirmation of the daring structure of time,
But we have watched long enough; let us descend
From the tall towers of vision and turn home,
We also, for where one went, others may go.'

Charles Brasch — *The Quest*

PART ONE
1944 — 1948
EARLY DAYS AND NEW PLAYS

The Compass Players can be seen as part of a theatre movement that existed in this country during and just after the war, helping to keep theatre alive at a time when theatre buildings in towns and cities were closing down or being destroyed by bombing. In 1940-41 the Council for the Encouragement of Music and the Arts (C.E.M.A.) started to provide support for companies who were willing to travel to theatreless towns and the hostels attached to munitions factories. The first of these companies was the Pilgrim Players and then shortly afterwards the Adelphi Players. A letter from the writer R. H. Ward, who was the founder of the Adelphi Players to his friend John Crockett, which was written from 38, Abbey Road, London, N.W.8, in February 1941 serves to remind the reader of those times:

'I walked through a number of streets behind Victoria the other day — Pimlico and Vauxhall Bridge Road way — and there it all was, the dreary, abject vileness of it: street after street of damaged houses; boarded windows like closed eyes; doors swinging unfastened; inside, the staircase in ruins, but the Woolworth shade still on the light-fitting in the hall. Some of the basements were inhabited; you could hear a trickle of music from the wireless seeping out from behind the wooden window-panes; troglodytes, less than human creatures, furtively living in holes, civilization ruined above them. I can't tell you the impression of sheer misery and foulness that those deserted streets made on me; it was like falling through hell. It was grey and lifeless and subhuman, a place of real horror. And then, in the midst of it all, at the end of Ebury St., the little dirty seventeenth-century house (once, I believe, a farm) in which Mozart composed his first symphony. Looking at it, reading the plaque on the wall, you wonder if you've gone mad. Imagine that precise, ordered, vital music arriving on paper there, in the midst of what is now chaos and deathliness. Wouldn't Mozart have gone mad if he could have looked forward a couple of centuries? It made it far worse, thinking of that particular kind of music, so luminous, in that shambles. And a little later, when it was getting towards evening, there were the subhuman

1

inhabitants of bombed London, shuffling out of their underground cellars, carrying bundles of bedding, and making for the Tube stations. Deep down in the earth in the only place where the only animal that goes on two legs can feel secure. And yet at the other extreme, we've discovered how to take ourselves miles up into the sky; but all we can do when we get there, Godlike creatures that we are, is shit bombs onto the cities beneath. Christ in heaven, what lunacy, what degradation and filthiness.

...I'd clear out now, if I could; but I can't either with a full pocket or a clear conscience. This seems to be the only place where we can earn our livings at our proper jobs, and the more I see of it, the more I know I've got to get this theatrical company going and cart it round these ghastly deserts if it kills me. I will not give in to the whole vile situation and pretend that things like the theatre have got to shut down because there's a war on, or that it's too difficult to do such a job in these conditions, or that nothing matters but the war, the war and again the war, and keeping out of the bomb's way...'

So Richard Ward went on to start his own theatre company. This has been described for us by Molly Sole, who was a founder member of Richard's company and also helped Compass and worked for the early mobile Century Theatre. She has always remained a dedicated theatre worker and in recent years she received an M.B.E. for her work for the Old Vic. She writes:

'At an Annual General Meeting of the Peace Pledge Union, held at the Cora Hotel as the Friends' Meeting House had been bombed, some time early in 1941 or perhaps late in 1940, a very tall man stood on a chair and said, "I am forming a group of travelling bakers; if anyone would like to join me please see me later." At least that is what I thought he said and this was confirmed by the fact that my companion who had been a teacher but was now a baker's delivery man (he was a conscientious objector and teachers were most often penalised) seemed very excited and went off to enquire further. However, it turned out that the project was for a band of Travelling Players and the man who made the announcement was Richard Ward who had been with the Pilgrim Players and had it in mind to start a third such, the other two being the Canterbury Pilgrims and the Oxford Pilgrims.

My friend came back full of the fact that the travelling company had enough actors but wanted a secretary and he had agreed to be just that and was off to a remote part of Essex in March to join up with the rest.

This jumps ahead a bit as it turned out that E.Martin Browne who was the director of the Pilgrim Players would not allow Richard to call his so far untried group another Pilgrim group until it had proved itself worthy. Coming to the rescue were Max Plowman and J.Middleton Murry who had a community settlement and farm at Boxted in Essex, mostly conducted in a large country house called 'The Oaks'. This was part of the set-up which published the prestigious *Adelphi* magazine and it was suggested that the acting group take the name also, as the principle of brotherly fair share for all was to be its basis — everyone having the same wage (£2 per week) and sharing all chores. At the Adelphi Centre were a number of refugees from the East End bombing, mostly elderly, some young mothers with their children and, for social occasions, various members of the farming community who were housed and worked from a farm down the road under the guidance of J. Middleton Murry (see his book *Community Farm*).

The Adelphi company went on increasing and expanding, moving up to the Potteries at one stage, along the Welsh valleys, to the Isle of Man in association with the Arts Council and finally came to rest permanently in Macclesfield touring the North West Region until the withdrawal of a crucial Arts Council grant brought its ten year life to an end.'

Richard Ward invited John Crockett to join his company which for a time he did, but although they always remained friends it was obviously difficult for two such strong personalities to work together for any length of time, and John also wished to develop his own ideas on theatre.

In the early months of 1943 John Crockett determined to find more ways of using music and, above all, dance, in the theatre productions and after discussions it was agreed that he should form an Adelphi Dance Company to start work in the autumn. This he set about doing and a programme was planned, dancers were engaged and the composer Peter Burden said he would join the company. C.E.M.A. agreed to support the venture if the dancers could get permits from the Ministry of Labour (several had come to England with the famous German company, 'Ballet Jooss'). The permits were not forthcoming and the project collapsed.

Anne Crockett, John's wife, was a dancer: in fact he often said, 'Anne and I met as dancers.' Anne explains this statement:

'We met when he had been persuaded to visit the Margaret Barr Dance Drama Group, of which I was a member. He was introduced to us by Freddy Manner, one of his teachers at Goldsmith College of Art. Freddy was the husband of one of the dancers. Margaret Barr had been one of Martha Graham's pupils in the United States and had come to England in 1928 where she had worked at Dartington. From Dartington she had come to London and formed a group of professional dancers who used the special technique of Martha Graham, based on the natural movements of the body, unlike ballet. She composed dance-dramas, and had the music composed specially for them, again unlike ballet where the opposite process takes place and the dance follows the music.

Zippa Weigall, who was a member of the dance drama group, has reminded me that three of her pianists and composers for her dance dramas became famous — Michael Tippett, Edward Rubbra and Alan Rawsthorne — and Theda da Moor was her leading dancer in London until she left to go back to South Africa at the beginning of the War. About the same time that

Margaret went to New Zealand after working with 'Labour Stage' at Unity Theatre.

Margaret Barr was the inspiration that led John and me to give dancing an important place in The Compass Players, the new company John started in 1944, and her kind of dancing, therefore, needs describing. She was the first practitioner of Graham technique in England, sometimes called the 'flat-footed' school (because the dancers were usually bare footed and never used block-toed ballet shoes). The foundation of the technique was that all movement started with the diaphragm with the intake of breath which was the impulse for the gesture to be shaped by the whole body. Maurice Browne, who produced many plays for The Compass Players and who had been the founder of the Chicago Little Theatre and a keen admirer of Stanislavsky and Gordon Craig, endorsed this idea. He always exhorted us to show by an intake of breath from the diaphragm the accent that started a movement or speech.

To return to our first meeting, John also told the following story; he told it many times and, if I heard him tell it, I was embarrassed, but also proud and pleased because he would say with pride and joy: "I walked into this hall (an old warehouse in Southwark) and there was this beautiful girl in a long blue dress with a crown and sceptre, and I fell in love." "He didn't have a chance!" I thought afterwards, with me being a personification of Imperialism in a drama called *The Red, White and Blue*. He was bowled over by my sceptre!'

After the failure of the Adelphi Dance Company John and Anne Crockett joined a small London company called the Masque Theatre. Its only production was a double bill, directed by Eileen Thorndike, consisting of Tchekov's The Bear *and a strange play by the fin de siècle Russian writer Evreinov,* A Merry Death, *which was written as a kind of dance drama.*

At this point it seems necessary to provide the reader with more insight into John Crockett's background and experience. He had been educated at Bryanston School in Dorset, a progressive public school where the Arts were nurtured and formed an important part of the curriculum. He then went to Goldsmith's College where he studied theatre design under V. Polunin, the artist who had painted the famous backcloths designed for Diaghelev by Picasso, Leger and others. He also attended classes at Michel St.Denis' London Theatre Studio. Later he became deeply involved with a progressive school for problem children — Little Missenden Abbey in Buckinghamshire, where he and the children would paint together freely with no formal teaching. It was here that he met his great friend, Charles Brasch, the New Zealand poet and writer who describes John in his memoir 'Indirections' *(O.U.P. 1980):*

'He was in violent revolt against his family's military tradition; his father was a regular army officer, his brother was destined for the army, and so had he been... He declared himself a communist; his paintings were full of caricatures of capitalists, priests and soldiers, stock figures of the time. He drew well, if rather too neatly and schematically... he was so possessed by waves of inarticulate rage against the world in general and especially his own upbringing that he seemed like those figures in the Gospels who fall to the ground incapable, foaming at the mouth, before Jesus drives the devil out of them.

John was at heart a gentle tender creature with a marked Franciscan strain of love for all creation, when he could allow this to express itself. He was extremely tall, about 6ft 4in, thin but strongly built, with well-made head and rather heavy cheeks, and large practical hands.

He was capable in many ways as actor, dancer, choreographer, designer, producer. But how was he to find an outlet for his energy and talent?'

This book will show how he found this outlet for the eight years of life of The Compass Players, the little company he was to form in 1944. Richard Ward wrote to him, 'Why don't you form your own theatre company? You know how to do it.' The Crocketts decided to do just that. John borrowed £150 as a capital start-up sum from an old friend, Douglas Robb, the rector of Deptford, a sum that was proudly repaid five years later. With this money a van had to be found, a London office established, a director of plays paid and equipment bought. It was decided to call the company THE COMPASS PLAYERS *and it was to run on a fully co-operative basis. The first urgent need was to find an actor who could also drive the van and had practical skills. Knowing and liking Leslie Hardie and* 'having every reason to know too his capacity for hard work and for laughter', *they invited him to join the company. Leslie has a clear recollection of events at that time and now, forty five years later, this has been invaluable in the writing of this chapter:*

'I first knew Anne Crockett at Wennington School in 1942. John, her husband, would come to visit her at weekends if Adelphi Players were performing within travelling distance. Suddenly John arrived one weekend with news of a crisis with Adelphi Players. Jesse Titcombe, their electrician, was sick (indeed lovesick) and was unable to continue working. John begged me to join Adelphi immediately as replacement electrician. They were touring along the South coast towards the West. Because the area of the coast was restricted it was necessary to have a C.E.M.A. identity card as well as the blue one that everyone had. It was pleasant touring with the Adelphi Players. At first I was apprehensive and rather withdrawn. A working-class chap among people who had a middle-class public school upbringing, yet there was a warmth of comradeship — a pride in doing a professional job together. I remember no rows or antagonisms. We were all much too busy.

Jack Boyd Brent, the director, was a mild-mannered, affable person. He had a slightly aloof pose as director. I remember him standing on the side, greatcoat slung over his shoulders watching the rest of us bustle around with our tasks. He would lend an unskilled languid hand if necessary but in the main he filled his position as director. In company meetings he would preside rather like an elder brother and ignore with some disdain any jokey interjection by lively youngsters like Piers Plowman.

At the end of the tour the company went to Ilkley to rehearse *Deidre of the Sorrows* by J. M. Synge. John Crockett came to design costumes and sets. Materials were short. Coupons had to be bargained for. The rich hangings of the sets and the elaborate costumes were a triumph of improvisation. We cut lino tiles with Celtic shapes (like *Book of Kells* designs); these were mounted on wooden blocks. A local printer supplied printing inks in bright colours. Long strips of hessian were laid in the theatre aisles. We inked the blocks with coloured designs and printed by placing them carefully and then jumping on them. I remember working long days making props and formulating lighting plots.

Jack Brent approached me one day with apologetic mien. "A terrible thing to ask," he said. Would I appear as one more spear-carrying soldier. I had no acting experience — I was even a reject for school plays. Sympathetic to the company's financial situation I agreed to stand in with reluctance. Maurice Browne was the producer, a very theatrical director of the old school, a little man with small beard and grand manner. He nabbed me one morning as we were alone in the theatre. "You are one of the soldiers, my boy. Let me hear your lines." I had but one. I had to dash in with the others and shout to Conchubor, the King (Jack Boyd Brent), "Eamon is in flames."

At Maurice's behest I stood and shouted my line where I stood. He looked at me with intense disgust. Modestly I opined, "That was a bit wet." "It was BLOODY WET!" he roared. "Get up on stage, get a spear, say it with meaning." Three or four tries produced no more satisfactory results. By this time the players were filtering in to make a growing audience to this painful farce. Eventually Maurice said firmly, "Take your spear. Go out of the theatre, run up the stairs, burst in the rear door of the auditorium and rouse us from our seats with the shout, 'Ilkley's in flames.'" I stood in the street summoning some possible latent talent. Finding no inspiration to assuage my despair I rushed up the stairs, flung open the door and shouted with loud passion, "Ilkley's in flames." The company turned their heads slowly from their seats in the front stalls. "Oh really?" they muttered. My performance must have improved sufficiently to play for the first weeks of the run.

John Crockett had discussions with me about the new company he wanted to form to do new plays by modern authors. From my "triumph" as a soldier he assumed that I would be able to act as well as look after the technical side — the transport, the driving, the lighting.'

Poor Leslie. The vans he had to cope with at that time were enough to break the spirit of the most experienced mechanical engineer; 'taking the Swift into a garage for petrol usually brought out the mechanics from the rear. They would ask to lift the bonnet to see the unique "scent spray" carburrettor. The brakes were adequate for an earlier era of motoring — pulled by cables that stretched and so became maladjusted. With the petrol tank above the engine we had a sudden fire three times.'

As John was the only map reader and Leslie the only driver, the actresses had to be crammed into the Swift first... incidentally, this conversion to a van of this 1929 Swift had a top speed of 30 m.p.h... they sat with their backs to the cab and the scenery and baggage was piled in on top of them. After the back flaps were tied the long-suffering actresses travelled everywhere sitting in the dark. Paula Burton (Rice) who joined the company in its early days recalls the next van which was a Black Maria:

'This was a police van, which was obviously built for heavy men with tall helmets. When it was collected by Leslie (our engineer driver) it turned over because it was so difficult to control with only one lightweight person in it. Luckily no damage was done to driver or vehicle, and apparently willing hands arrived from somewhere to help put them back on the road. Poor Anne, who suffered from claustrophobia, was packed in in the wrong way in one of our vans, with the result that, when she was released, after hours of being hemmed in by all the theatrical paraphernalia, she relieved her pent-up emotional fears by bursting out of the back of the van swearing like a trooper into the arms of the kindly vicar who had come to welcome us! By the time I left the company we had about seven members and a bus, and by this time Anne had learnt to drive. Almost always we could drive right up to the stage doors to unload, but there was at least one occasion when there was only a narrow passage to unload in and we had to carry our things through the streets of a town. The real trouble for us during the War was that no-one wanted to give strangers information, especially about direction, in case they were spies. Not only that, to add to our perplexities, country folk in remote districts would often alter signposts, pointing them in the opposite directions — to confuse the enemy! A good map-reader was an essential person and John always did that job, and he did it well as we always got to our destinations on time.'

Leslie goes on to describe the other vehicles which are now obviously indelibly printed on to his memory:

'Our next vehicle, needed to transport an enlarged company and more equipment, was an ex-mobile operating theatre on a Leyland Cub chassis. This vehicle was called Poots because there was a gown on a hook with a label 'Dr Poots'.

Poots was a spacious, luxurious vehicle for us. Passengers were no longer uncomfortably crammed in with baggage. It was a dull khaki coloured monster but John painted 'Compass Players' in large white letters on each side which gave it a new identity. I had to buy the vehicle at a distance, having once seen it in London. The A.A. had vetted it and handed it over to some mechanics in a railway arch in Bethnal Green. On the advice of the A.A. they had rewired the ignition system — I felt unnecessarily — but failed to discover a cracked cylinder block which gave trouble later. I only had a hint of it when I discovered a used tin of Wonderworld (a product that would bung up cracks from within — temporarily). Nevertheless, Poots served us well for a few months until Adelphi II gave us the original Adelphi bus.

This was an A.E.C. luxury giant that had seen its best days on the Royal Blue run between London and Bournemouth in the '30s. The driver had to sit in a separate cabin over the engine of huge size and deafening noise. Passengers travelled in armchair luxury while the driver suffered howling draughts through the pedal holes in the wooden floorboards. Communication was through a hosepipe with funnel ends. Although this emerged by the driver's ear, shouted navigational instructions were almost impossible to hear. John, as navigator, used to get angry with me when we went off course.

Modern motorists take their convenient and comfortable cars and commercial vehicles for granted and do not realise the slow advance of technical progress between the early years of the century and the late '40s. Starting was a ritual that had to be commenced long before the company had the morning call to travel. Before anti-freeze was available engines and radiators had to be drained overnight if there was a hint of frost. The bottom third of the radiator had to be blocked with a sheet of cardboard to prevent cold air freezing the radiator when the fan pulled air through initially. The Black Maria was the only vehicle to have a self starter. Each engine had to have idiosyncracies of its starting understood. The right position of the swing, the setting of ignition and choke. It must be remembered that this was the age of magneto ignition. Very often the gentle touch of a little actress on the advance/retard lever was a vital element in starting.

Advice from experts was universal. STARTING was a topic of conversation among motorists as weather is now. 'Oh, you have a Leyland. Before you try and start in the morning tip out the contents of the carburretor float chamber — it collects condensation overnight.' It worked! Swinging an engine to start required strength as well as skill. Frequently the handle did not free quickly, resulting in a wrenched shoulder and knuckles lacerated on the honeycombed radiator. I had to make up my hands for the stage to hide grazes. The scars are still there.

The Adelphi bus was a splendid vehicle but it had various technical faults. It had no self-starter, no speedometer — so we did not know how far and fast we were driving. I tested speed over a measured stretch and averaged 50m.p.h. at top speed. Petrol consumption was about 5m.p.g. officially, actually we got over 10m.p.g. Fiddling was necessary because some local fuel officers could be mean with petrol coupons.

The bus clutch was held by two stretched cables which would snap under strain. I carried spares for quick replacement. Once I had to drive from Abergavenny to our home base in Gloucestershire without a clutch. By then I could crash the gears through without mishap. Learning to 'double declutch' before the days of syncromesh gave the bonus of added facility.

Sometimes the 'autovac' which syphoned petrol from tank to carburretor would give up, and remedial action had to be taken en route to restore its function. Driving the bus required skill but Phoebe Waterfield of Adelphi II had a sure, adroit touch. Although slight and feminine, she drove the cumbersome vehicle with great aplomb. We agreed that it was a most demanding but satisfying vehicle to drive.

The rear seats were removed to carry skips, lighting and baggage. Front seats were well spaced so that passengers could stretch out in comfort (modern coaches have less comfortable seating). Flats were carried in a box-like container on the roof. I remember Wilfred Harrison stating in company meeting that it should be one person's responsibility to pack the flats. He got the job. I remember Wilfred standing on the roof in driving rain struggling with flats, not daring to complain.

Coming south through Ludlow, an Austin 7 came skidding towards me on the icy road. As I swerved to avoid it I grazed a house on my nearside. Our service garage at Hereford decreed that the bus was a write-off because the roof had shifted. However, the insurance company paid out £400 on the bus and Compass Players — no longer with me — were able to buy a decent vehicle.'

Even today the van is the centre of any travelling theatre company's life. The actors may have to go without food but the van must always have its petrol and oil. But to move on now to the new company's productions.

The director of the first production was Maurice Browne, who in semi-retirement now directed for both the Adelphi Players and The Compass Players. John Crockett said of him: 'He had a very great genius for getting incredible depths of feeling from those he was producing and could be quite ruthless to anyone who showed insincerity in rehearsal.' *He proposed that the first play should be a new one, written in verse by the Georgian poet Wilfred Wilson Gibson who also happened to be a friend of his. It was called* 'Ernshaw', *and was not a great success, as Leslie describes for us:*

'Ernshaw, Compass's first production was rehearsed in the village hall behind the pub at Winsford where Maurice Browne lived with his assistant producer and minder, Molly Underwood. I found her insights a great help in discussing interpretation but Maurice exaggerated her gifts because he loved her dearly. Maurice's sister also lived with us in the house; she had been Harold Munro's wife and treated us with rather lofty disdain. *Ernshaw* in my opinion was a dull little play. It was in verse and John was very keen on verse plays. Nobody in the audiences seemed to realise that *Ernshaw* was in verse. Action was early 'kitchen sink'!'

The play, although in three acts, did not last much longer than an hour and so The Bear *was added as a curtain raiser and later Laurence Housman's* Abraham and Isaac *was included in the repertoire. The next production was again a new play, this time written by R. H. Ward and called* The Secret Life. *Although it was far from perfect John Crockett felt that it was a big step forward for The*

Compass Players because it dealt with subjects that mattered — 'Social, in that it was an attack on the rich and selfish landowners. Psychological, in that it dealt with the secret life that hid the reality of the outwardly respectable.' *It was kept in the repertory for about a year and was surprisingly successful, particularly with all sorts of Forces audiences.*

Leslie's recollections are hilarious:

'It concerned an odd group of people marooned by flood on a landing in a large country house. We all had to simulate coming upstairs behind a solid bannister and newel post downstage. So good were we at rising gradually from our knees behind this unique piece of scenery that many an organiser was worried that we would make good the hole that we had cut in their stage. Maurice Browne produced the play as a wholly dramatic clash of personality, class and generation. After a few months Richard Ward caught up with us on tour in the Town Hall in Penzance. 'I did not mean it to be interpreted in this way,' he stated, aghast. Consequently, the play was retimed and re-rehearsed to turn it into a comedy. Playing the same lines for laughs was a strange experience. The play went down much better. I remember Maurice's original striving for dramatic effect. Lady Enn was trying to seduce me in the rather oblique manner permissable at that period. Maurice instructed me, 'What I want from you is to turn on her, lift up her dress and shout "cunt". Of course you cannot do it literally, but that is the effect I want.' The visual impact of the cast of *The Secret Life* must have been confusing for an audience. John and Anne, the tall landed gentry, the Enns. Paula the housekeeper and Zita as Miss Dropper — both about 5ft. — and myself as Angel, the prig of doubtful parentage somewhat in between. Miss Dropper sat for most of the action making pithy philosophical remarks while John and I fought the class/generation war across the stage. Once I got a cheer from a partisan South Wales audience who supported my standpoint. It is doubtful whether any company will want to revive *The Secret Life,* but it did break new ground. Given a wider showing it might have been a turning point in British theatre as *Look Back in Anger* was later. Most British plays at that time seemed to be middle-class drawing-room comedies with any working-class character inarticulate and comic.

By the time we were putting *The Secret Life* into the repertoire Michael MacOwen was head of drama at C.E.M.A. I asked what he had done to become in such an exalted position. I was told that his father had been famous in the theatre establishment and that he had done pioneer work in the Forces with 'living newspaper' productions. He did little for us despite the respect that was shown him. He borrowed our vehicle to take his children on a jaunt around Devon and used our spare petrol. A phone call told us that he had managed to break the half-shafts. I remember frustrating my annoyance. However, we did not gain much from our entertaining. A list of booking agents in the South West, C.E.M.A. commissioned a play for us and engaged a producer, Richard Scott, who had had success with The

Torch Theatre in London doing experimental plays. The commissioned play was *The Cockleshell*, a contemporary drama dealing with a family in the war-time situation.'

The Cockleshell *was written by the actor Wilfred Walter who had also written a successful two-hander before the war called* Happy and Glorious. *It was an ingenious portrait of the war that had just ended. Multi-scened with extremely economical dialogue and with, as commentators to the action, a good angel and a demon king on either side of the stage. The demon king also had to impersonate Neville Chamberlain, Churchill and Montgomery amongst others. The scenes included a munitions factory, a workers' home, waiting for the start of the battle of El Alamein, an exterior of a Nazi prison, and a devastated Germany. Towards the end of the play the demon king sets off the atom bomb — possibly the first time (1946) that the atom bomb had been treated in English theatre. The play was vitiated only by the weakness of its finale where the family, survivors of the war, are constructing the boat* The Cockleshell — *a symbol of freedom and harmony. John Crockett wrote:* '...the technique of the play brought the realisation that it was possible, under touring conditions, to present a multi-scene production and that a play performed by relatively few actors playing many different parts is acceptable to a British audience.' *Leslie Hardie continues:*

'Halfway through rehearsals Richard Scott, in some despair, confided in me that he was on the point of resigning as producer. His main concern was that John would not take direction and felt that *his* interpretation should prevail. We discussed the consequences of such an action on his part — the effect on the company, the impression that C.E.M.A. would get, but above all the artistic damage to the production. Richard Scott was persuaded to continue directing, but his heart was not in it. *The Cockleshell* was staged in a draped set. Rapid scene changes were achieved with rostra, cut outs, folded scenery and, above all, lighting.

The play itself was quite well received because it was different and had the impact of the current situation. The most vivid memory for me was a particular performance when during a rapid scene change a large long rostrum had to be raised to provide an escarpment for me to scale as a soldier with a rifle in one hand. I had to throw myself to grasp the highest corner and haul myself up with the other hand. Paula and Zita were underneath holding the rostrum but had failed to put the supporting strut into place. I could hear their distress as they tried to hold the heavy rostrum with me on top of it. All I could do was make the noise of a shot and drop off with a thud on to the stage. People came round after the show and said that the effect was startling. However, we did not keep it in both for my sake and risked bruising and Paula's and Zita's peace of mind. *The Cockleshell* did break new ground in production techniques and subject matter, but I doubt its revival. Revival of many of the early productions of Compass Players may be doubtful, but I am sure that any reader of *The Quest* by Charles Brasch will want to re-read the splendid poetry of the piece.

Charles Brasch, an old friend of John Crockett, was a New Zealand poet of international status. His verse appears in several anthologies. He was one of the quietest, modest and kindly of men. He was short, dark and had a middle-eastern appearance. His serious manner and thoughtful mien could burst into smiling appreciation of fun. I well remember one occasion, a hot day in high summer. We drove past Malham Tarn. Spontaneously we stopped our vehicle and all Compasses flung off their clothes and dived into the water. Except Charles who looked on with more amusement than embarrassment. Several times during his writing of *The Quest* he came to visit us on tour to discuss with John. The whole play was written in very well-crafted verse. We spoke as various solo characters around the main player who was a young man making a difficult physical and spiritual journey. The action was punctuated by stanzas of verse spoken in unison by the whole company.

To achieve the highest possible standard of performance in both verse speaking and dance, rehearsal was rigorous and painstaking in detail. Every morning before breakfast Anne 'schooled' us in ballet exercises. Efforts were rewarded when, after a week at The Everyman Theatre at Cheltenham a critic wrote:

'The standard of The Compass Players' dance would have done credit to a full-time ballet company.' '

The Quest was directed by Richard Ward who had considerable experience of working with verse drama and the complexities of choral speech. He plotted the basic movements but the full design of every mime and dance was choreographed by Anne Crockett and Paula Rice.

Sadly Charles Brasch never saw The Quest *produced as he returned to his native New Zealand shortly before the first performance.*

For The Cockleshell *and* The Quest *the company had been considerably enlarged from its original 2 actors and 3 actresses. Leslie Hardie now goes on to describe them all:*

'For Compass Players John Crockett was the dominant figure. He was the founder, man of ideas who generated the artistic energy. Earlier he had injured his back and had a 'patent' welding job done by an eminent surgeon a Mr Cyriax. Therefore, John could not do much lifting and carrying. He always had a sketch book to hand. People, places, equipment, beds all were recorded. Although believing in democracy in the form of company meetings about policy and finance John was basically an autocrat. Finances were tight and I can remember we had to state what luxuries we could hardly do without. John insisted on suits made by his West End tailor (the director had to present a good appearance and only *that* tailor could make proper pockets). John had to have his packet of 20 Gold Flake a day and his tin of Mick McQuaid plus his annual subscription to the London Library had to be maintained. I settled for the occasional pint of beer. The girls' needs were also very modest. John had been with the Adelphi's but had found day to day work with them insupportable. Friendship remained and there was a closeness with brother companies but I felt that John would be unhappy unless he were the director. At first we were three. *Ernshaw* demanded two more women so Paula Rice and Zita Jenner joined us.

Anne Stern (Crockett) was the senior, director's wife, secretary and treasurer. I had known her at Wennington as a very able and accomplished music teacher and pianist. Anne was the back-bone of the common sense in the company. She had a London sense of humour. Mistress of the concise telling phrase, the sharp observation after which she would pull in her lips tightly and leave a silence so that the remark sunk in. Anne would make the best of any bad situation with lugubrious resignation.. Tough she was but I have known her weak with tender emotion. She looked beautiful, smart and serene whatever the circumstances.

Paula Rice was a graduate of the Ginner Mawer School of Dance and Drama. She was a small, graceful and gracious person, her future as an actress was restricted by her lack of height — 5' 1"? Paula was accommodation officer, she booked our lodgings in advance. Her letters had to be vetted by John because her spelling was a bit suspect. One organiser was asked where we could put our 'vehile'. Paula's concern for our welfare was all-embracing. She had a well-maintained store of food and drink in a couple of shopping bags which she lugged around on all occasions. If any of us wilted she had the means to sustain us. She made cups of tea whenever we arrived at a venue after a journey. She had the minimum of wants or needs. I still have a picture of her in her black and white checked wintercoat. Fair hair pulled back over her fresh, newly-washed round face — always cheerful, always content and pleasant to all. Paula eschewed personal comfort, wore no stockings, sensible school-type shoes, no gloves even in bitter weather. She had great artistic integrity and was capable of quietly putting her point of view to John on artistic interpretation. She even told Maurice Brown that his play *Job* was weak. He was not pleased.

Zita Jenner was also a little girl. Very conventional with a conservative convent school upbringing she was quite as capable as the rest of us in braving the conditions and the occasional poverty. Sometimes we were down to our last shillings and were even hungry. Once in Derby we all went into a café and had to toss up to find who would have the soup, the entree or the sweet. We had three meals between the five of us. Zita was amazing in her ready acceptance of the change from a comfortable middle-class life. She was an actress of some versatility. Among her roles was my long-suffering wife in *Ernshaw*, the farmer's wife in Hans Sachs' *Strolling Clerk*, Miss Dropper in the *Secret Life*, again Mrs. Bumpus to my Mr Bumpus in *How He Lied to her Husband*, etc. A character actress who would work hard on any role offered. She was also a very dedicated wardrobe mistress always cleaning, washing and repairing under the difficult conditions of travelling.

Zita's height was similar to Paula's but she had a good clear carrying voice and was very patient at taking direction.

As we put on programmes demanding more players others joined us, Paul Oliver, a Londoner, with Irish Italian forebears, was one. With his cockney accent and his native-Soho intelligence and warmth he was a pleasant comrade. He was a willing, helpful, modest participant in all areas of the company's work. The only time I saw him angry was when John got at him in a company meeting. In frustration Paul smashed his fist down on the table. He had a bad gash on the side of his hand. I remember particularly Paul's patient training and practice to eliminate some cockney speech trends so that his verse speaking was congruent with ours for the choruses in unison in *The Quest*. Paul had a great capacity for the uncomplicated enjoyment of life. He enjoyed food, comradeship in the company, he danced with zest and in later years John described how he belted into the Catholic litany with great verve. No run-of-the-mill extrovert, he could be withdrawn, even moody but always sensitive to others' feelings.

Maurice Daniels came to us in 1946 with a deal of experience of producing theatricals in the Congo where he had worked as an executive for Lever. He was a kind and sensitive man who was prepared to work hard and help with any task. To every area of our joint effort that required intelligence and thought he would apply his fine mind and cultivated sensitivity. He had a rich acting voice and a characteristic, rather stiff movement and stance. Normally a quiet man, he had a sudden Ho! Ho! Ho! laugh when something funny happened. A fluent French speaker, he made one very unusual performance possible. Because Dover had been bombarded during the war the Belgians sent a large group of workmen over to help repair damage to the town. It was a gesture of goodwill not appreciated entirely by the local Council. The men who came were painstaking craftsmen who were slower and were paid higher rates than the local Council workmen. Our visit to Dover happened to coincide with civic junketing of goodwill with visiting Belgian dignitaries. We were asked to put on a sort of gala performance. The programme was changed to an amended 'schools' programme' to provide more action than words. Maurice provided commentary and impromptu translation of dialogue for the whole performance. At the curtain call we stood in line while speeches were made in French and English — Maurice still translating. To our embarrassment large bunches of flowers were presented to each of us. 'Artists so talented and so young!'

Elizabeth Wright joined us for *The Quest*, an experienced actress who had been with Donald Wolfit's company. A quiet professional, she spoke verse well, moved with grace and was a well liked member of the company who gave great help with practical matters such as stage management and wardrobe.

Wilfred Harrison was a very welcome Compass member when Adelphi II folded. I remember what a relief it was to have skilled help with driving and electrical rigging. Easily he was the most impressive member of the company. Wilfred was 6' 4" with a head of curly auburn hair and 'a mighty organ' of a voice. His Halifax accent was not apparent unless he was speaking conversationally. He was a very even-tempered stabilizing influence. He was only angry with me once over a professional lapse. I dried on an entrance in *Box and Cox* on a visual cue that I had missed. Wilfred leaned over his stove, cooking his bacon, muttering loudly, 'Come on, yer bugger.' In later years Wilfred, after he left Century Theatre for which he raised money, acted and directed, became director of Bolton Octagon Theatre.

Christina Megroz came of a literary family and was well grounded in theatrical lore and plays, having worked with Anne Casson and the Osiris Players. She had great concern for people's welfare and would express herself earnestly in her delightful plummy voice. Christina's mother would be sent her dirty washing by post and it would return clean the following week. One week the dirty washing was not received and assumed lost in the post. Weeks later an irate letter came from Christina's elder sister on the staff of the Madrid Embassy. She had received a parcel of dirty washing in the Diplomatic Bag, because a previously used wrapping with a second label had been sent through the Central Sorting Office in London.

Brian Stapleton, whom I had known in an ambulance unit early in the war, came to join Compass in the last months of 1945. He was to play small roles and help generally. Very keen he was to drive and I remember giving him some tuition, and his execution of 'bunny hops' with the Black Maria, a difficult vehicle to keep on course, with a vicious clutch. By that time we were very busy with schools' programmes plus evening shows, sometimes at different venues. We were very glad of Brian's all-round help. Later he gained an Economics degree at L.S.E. and became a lecturer in African Universities, mainly in Nigeria. He was the Quaker representative in Brussels for UNESCO from 1979-83.

Advance booking was a job that did not invite prolonged application because it meant isolation. Initially the Compass tours' manager was a man of presence and gravity named Mike Pelham. He failed to take off because he decided to marry suddenly and we were left without bookings to start our first tour with *Ernshaw* and *Abraham and Isaac*. As I had but a small villainous part I was sent to secure some bookings. I approached local authorities, education committees, army camps, government hostels, churches, women's guilds, *etc*. It was hard and disappointing work selling an unknown company with unknown plays to people unacquainted with live theatre. It was the least happy job in the company.'

Brian Stapleton stepped into the role of Tours' Manager because no-one else was available and someone had to do the job, so he volunteered and 'was immediately Hobson's Choice.' *He describes the unenviable task:*

'This was a lonely road with few jackpots in sight. Forces' units were disbanding, no longer offering easy pickings; Education Authorities were nervous of committing scarce resources; local amateur companies were on short commons; no-one owed us a living. Somehow, often with the aid of stalwart "old friends" of the Company, I managed to string together a pattern of dates without too many wild swings from one area to another. A few on the Welsh borders just saved us — the Company bus staggered through the snow just before Wales was cut off for almost a week. That winter of '46-'47 was rough, one of the coldest this century. With money short I hitched much of the time, sometimes being picked up because I looked as if I could wield a spade should need arise — and it did once or twice crossing the Cotswolds.

I bought my two eggs and half-ounce of butter, hitched and walked back to The Warren (our rehearsal base) and shared them with whoever was in charge. Now and again I managed to meet up with the Company but lived in constant fear of them meeting up with me. Were they to do so and I had to confess "there is NO DATE tomorrow, or tomorrow, or..." it would spell mutual disaster.

I developed new skills — the ability to write legible, careful letters in a busy Post Office; to chat lengthily and persuasively from a phone box, ignoring water up to my ankles and a bitter wind howling up my legs; pretending to be 'the big people from London' who just happened to be passsing through. Now and again all the effort seemed worth it. One bitter evening I was travelling on a worker's bus in South Wales listening to a conversation in the seat in front: "Going to the theatre tonight, boyo?" "Dunno." "It's the Compass Players, I'm going; always do something good, maybe a bit strange but good acting."

Although the play was THE thing and the show always had to go on in order that we could eat, we did take time out for what Anne referred to as "a drop of culture" any time there was a chance — Lincoln, Ely, those beautiful cathedrals and many lesser buildings, art exhibitions, bookshops, my education was continuing. Perhaps luckily there are very few Compass Inns, but we insisted on calling any time we found one.

John lectured us on neatness and tidiness of person. Setting forth again to conquer Wales we reckoned we looked like a set of bank clerks, to be greeted by the headmistress of Abergavenny Girls School, "Oh, how delightfully Bohemian you all look"... Later, when we had the bus, John suggested painting a series of glamorous actors and actresses along the windows... but we all wanted to be able to look out, if we were awake. We found a lot of enthusiastic audiences in the Valleys — many of the old Welfare Halls with excellent stages. Digs were poor and food difficult to come by — even cooking facilities. Paula once just went knocking on doors with a full frying pan in her hands. When I became Tours Manager the Director of Education of one Welsh County set a trap for me — "and 'ow do you find Welsh audiences, Mr. Stapleton?' Well, er, they are very responsive... (and, ever the innocent) they don't object to a little overacting"." We OVERACT in REAL LIFE by your standards!!"

Half an hour to curtain up; lighting plot not finished; stage curtain working badly; someone lost someone else's make-up, in comes our hostess: "Just like the GOOD COMPANIONS!"

Well, we were, but the real life lesson we all learned was how to live together and get the show on every night.

After Brian, two very attractive actresses took over the booking of tours — Josephine Jemmett and Catherine Dunoon — and worked together with some success. Leslie continues:

'Periodically they came to visit the company to report progress and receive guidance and also to see performances to be able to describe shows to possible bookers. Out of the blue we received a telegram which read "BABOON AND BABETTE ARRIVING TUESDAY". We expected a novelty act to tack on to the school's programme but it was only really Dunoon and Jemmett. Josephine on a booking tour in Lanarkshire became friendly with a Miss Hamilton who was preparing to open a newly refurbished hotel as manageress. She invited the company to make use of the hotel before it opened. When we availed ourselves of her generous offer we realised very quickly that Miss Hamilton was disenchanted with us. With dismay she viewed Paula's bags of provender. At the end of a week she was following us with brush and dustpan moaning, "The crumbs, oh, the crumbs." By then I was the only one on speaking terms with her. To cause her less agony because she was in a state of nervous terror of us, we agreed to leave the next day as 12 noon. At about 11 a.m. John dropped part of his Gillette razor down the large Victorian plug-hole of the wash basin. It was of sentimental value to him because it had belonged to his father and was gold-plated. We tried all means of recovery — wire, magnets, poking things through the trap — nothing would move it. Eventually I had to take the wash basin off the wall and shake it. I just got it back in place as Miss Hamilton opened the room door to speed our much desired departure. A few seconds before she would have been dissolving in nervous hysteria...'

Leslie goes on to describe some of the accommodation the Company had on tour which could range from 'the depth of crumminess to the height of opulence.' Much of it was hospitality from kind members of the audience but when that was not available it was occasionally necessary to find a hotel:

'The lowest point ever was Fox's Private Commercial Hotel at Barnsley. Because we gave three shows in the day we could not go to the place that the Council had booked for us. Exhausted, we knocked at the hotel door at midnight. We were told that we would be expected and that a deposit of half cost had been paid. After banging for about five minutes the door opened on a chain. A hand came out of the crack and a surly Yorkshire voice demanded, 'Oos paying?' In the rain and blackout we all fumbled through our pockets and just about found the amount asked before we were admitted to the filthiest rooms imaginable. Crumbs and fluff littered the bedroom floor and, tired as we were, the beds looked far from inviting. We were informed that breakfast was at eight and that we had better be on time. Punctually, we were waiting in the dingy passage for the dining room door to be unpadlocked. Once in the dining room, the elderly, unshaven, unsavoury proprietor unlocked the sideboard drawers, also fitted with hasps and padlocks, to throw some worn cutlery on the table for us. "I know what you theatrical people are like," he snarled. The breakfast was such that I have erased it from my memory.

At the other extreme we were entertained in stately homes. While working on advance booking I was guest overnight at Chatsworth. My position in society decreed that the chief housekeeper should look after me. All was very proper — even ceremonial. I was shown the splendid theatre, 18th-century splendour with gilded boxes heavily ornamented with all the original backstage machinery. I stopped to look in wonder. 'That is the very spot where an actress smacked King Edward VII when he pinched her bottom,' I was told.

Another delightful house to visit was The Manor at Redmire — the home of the Burrill-Robinsons. Half the beautifully-proportioned rooms were closed because the servants had long since gone. The Burrill-Robinsons invited us to use their home as a base whenever we played in the Yorkshire dales. There we spent some of our happiest times. They were such kind and convivial people. We all pitched in with the household chores, and meals around the big kitchen table were hilarious. I asked them if they did not look back nostalgically to the gracious days of the high living gentry. 'No,' they said. 'Dressing for dinner every evening with servants standing behind each chair watching to serve our every need. No, now is the best time of our life.' Henrietta Burrill-Robinson had been one of the "bright young things" of the '20s. She had danced with the Ballet Russe and raced cars at Brooklands — the first woman racing driver. Her "special" still stood in the garage on blocks. In those days her young mechanic had been Jack Warner, later Dixon of Dock Green. She was a painter of great talent, a member of the Redmire coterie of artists. She also was a keen and able mechanic. Many years later I visited the house and their graves in the churchyard. The house is now let for holiday makers with flatlets in the outhouses. We managed to stay overnight in the splendid bedroom I knew from the past. As I looked across the park there was quiet joy within me remembering past happy days. "Have you any of her paintings?", I was asked. "They are worth much."

Although the Scottish tour of 1945 was a disaster financially there were episodes of heartwarming hospitality that are vivid in my memory. At Kirkcudbright I went to collect the key to the town hall. The door was opened by a short, broad lady who was made more so by a voluminous black cloak and a broad-brimmed black Spanish hat. She did not answer my enquiry immediately but gazed into my eyes. "I can see that you are the sort of person that sees the fairies! Come with me." She led me through the house to a seat behind the hedge at the bottom of the garden. "You sit there while I make a cup of tea for us. With luck we may see the little folk." Eagerly, on her return, she asked if I had seen them. I had to admit that I was not sensitive to their presence that day. Next day she invited me to bring my girlfriend to dinner. "I will serve you dinner in the smallest dining room in Scotland." It was true, had we been larger — Paula and I — we could not have sat in that tiny room under the staircase.

Ern and Jessie Taylor were both artists of great merit. He had pictures in the Scottish Academy in Edinburgh — mainly Highland landscapes deeply outlined with fresh colours. Jessie was a book illustrator. She did fantastic, graceful beautifully detailed pictures of fairies and elves. Her works are very sought after by book collectors. I still can see in my mind all the Compasses playing with the Taylor's multifarious collection of children's toys — wonderful wooden mechanicals. Crocodiles that snapped, snakes that wiggled, dolls that nodded. We were happy children for the morning.

We hit Scotland during the V.E. Day celebrations. Our dramatic offerings did not form a part of anybody's shenanigins. Audiences were so small in places like Dalbeatie that company outnumbered "the house" and we deliberated about playing. (I remember Maurice Browne saying that if there was but one person in an audience that was affected it was worth the effort.) I doubted if there was "one" many times in Scotland. So hard up were we that we resorted to Youth Hostels for accommodation. As the only member of Y.H.A., I was usually sent in first to parley with the warden and convince him that the whole company should be taken in. We always succeeded in persuading the breakage of rules about individual membership and duration of stay. A week of lapsed bookings and nowhere to go landed us in a hostel in the Galloway moors. The warden was very suspicious and taciturn to begin with, but by the end of a week his family and Compasses were a happy community. Mrs. Warden did some delightful Scottish cooking for us all and two lads collected vast quantities of gulls' eggs for huge omelettes. Such hospitality merited a special gala performance. Warm embraces on our departure contrasted with our cold reception a few days before.

Scotland was no different in variation of accommodation from other parts of the country. There were dingy hotels and splendid private hospitality. One remembers the bad and the good. We did morning school performances in Govan. The whole school population must have been there. We had to strike with great despatch to set up in Marchline. On arrival there I was met by Mrs Corrie, wife of Joe Corrie, author of kitchen comedies and Glasgow newspaper columnist. She took me to task at first sight. "I see traces of make-up in your hair. How do you expect people to have any respect for actors if you are so dirty?" I explained that I had been madly busy since early morning, but it had no effect. During the whole of my stay she nagged about one thing or another. Especially when I arrived home with her husband at midnight after some very convivial late drinking in Burns' favourite pub "Pudsey Nancy's". Next morning Mrs Corrie told me that I did not know what it was to try to bring up a family with a husband who was a working-class author. I didn't — but I have a better appreciation — Burns' women must have suffered too.

Near Moffat — on the road to St Mary's Loch — a wonderfully hospitable couple kept a youth hostel. They had retired from keeping a grocery shop in Dundee. Having no children they decided that they must do "something for youngsters" in their declining years. Their first impression on one was of grim dourness, but that was a sort of shyness. Once at ease, they were the kindest of folk. Arriving at night cold and wet we were welcomed to their kitchen to a warm fire and a great bowl of broth. Every traveller who passed was offered a cup of tea. One day, seeing a platoon of soldiers sitting on the front lawn, I asked how it was done when tea was strictly rationed. "Don't you worry about that my son, the Lord provides." We helped the Lord by sending on unused Compass tea coupons.'

There were of course other touring theatre companies travelling round Britain at this time, for the tradition of barnstorming theatre has always been part of our cultural heritage. The standards were very variable and ranged from the C.E.M.A./Arts Council sponsored tours to very basic fit-up theatre. Leslie remembers several of them:

'On tour we met with colleagues of other companies. I remember several pleasant liaisons with Sadlers Wells Opera. They visited us in the Midlands when they were in Coventry and in return I visited Sadlers Wells to see the first production of Benjamin Britten's *Peter Grimes*. We also had warm and friendly encounters with The Osiris Players — an all-women group who travelled in ancient Rolls Royces and would perform the whole of Shakespeare to order. Each actress would play many parts, on and off stage so quickly that they had to indicate change of character by merely doffing another hat. I remember talking to a very appealing, down-trodden little actress who seemed to be in abject exhausted despair with the demanding régime that the Osiris followed.

Another touching liaison was with a company in deepest Wales. They relinquished the village hall during a week of playing to allow us in for a one night stand. For that evening they were our guests and sat in the front row dressed in their "Sunday best" for the occasion. They were gentle kindly people who toured remote Wales with such productions as *Smilin' Through*, *Sweeney Todd* and *Charley's Aunt*. Their lighting was much more primitive than ours although they billed their performance as "spectacular and scientific". We had a convivial meal with them after our performance. Modestly and sweetly they admired our set-up and performance. On a shelf in the dressing room we found their script of Charley's Aunt painstakingly written in an exercise book. (I met similar companies from a past age of

isses Rice, Stern, Jenner. Messrs Hardie, Crockett in Maria, Creetown, 1945.

Maria's contents.

Maria and trailer, Goathland. Yorks. This hall was lit by gas and oil lamps, 1945.

V.E. Night, Balmimnoch. May, 1945.

A Paula picnic. Miss Denoon in foreground, L. Hardie towards her.

All for Truth. *A new version by P. D. Cummins of* Le Misanthrope *by Molière.* *1949*

Dressing room. Ravenstruther Public Hall, Lanark, 24.5.45. It was in this village that a dance was to be organised after the show to help raise money for us. Not a single person turned up for it, and the 3-piece band arrived rather merry. They had to be paid.

The Quest

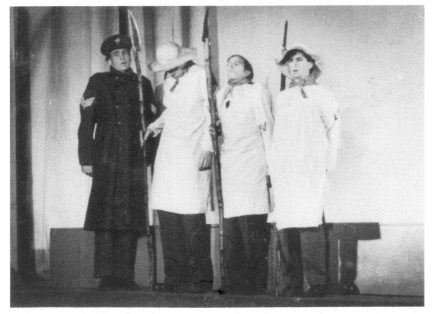

The Cockleshell

23

Pierrot Columbine and Harlequin. John Crockett oil/canvas, 1946.

Harlequin, Columbine and Pierrot. John Crockett oil/canvas, 1947.

Creation, John Crockett oil/canvas, 1948.

John Crockett, self portrait c.1940.

Anne 1939.

The painting by John Crockett depicts the stage right wings of the stage in a giant Nissen hut somewhere in the wilds of Norfolk. This was the theatre for a large army camp in the spring of 1944. Encamped there, secretly, was the Eighth Army (the famous Desert Rats) who were preparing to take part in the invasion of France on D Day. The company was enjoined to secrecy, as publicly, for the information of the enemy, this army was said to be out of the country. The performance in progress was of Turgenev's The Bachelor in what was a new English translation by the twin brothers Quinton and was the first production in this country of the play. The performers were the Adelphi Guild Theatre (formerly the Adelphi Players), the production was by Maurice Browne, costumes by John Crockett. In the painting are, in the foreground Jane Fitzgerald, Greta Newell on prompt, and Piers Plowman.

barnstorming in Ireland also.) Unchronicled remnants of a past age — not recognising themselves as perpetrators of the Celtic oral tradition. Their playbills listed a different play every night! We regretted that we had to move on and could not see them perform.

Another group was a throwback to a past era. They were an ex-E.N.S.A. company that had toured the recently warring world with a comedy *Without The Prince*. They had translated their E.N.S.A. régime to their own private enterprise. The following week the company folded in economic disaster. We discussed their plight with them and they agreed that they might have survived with our co-operative economics. The actresses were rather like pathetic mem-sahibs with long cigarette holders. They employed stage and wardrobe staff. Their bus was a rather grand one with shining buff paintwork and beautifully lined. (They admitted that they had paid far too much for it.) A chauffeur drove them. Their ex-E.N.S.A. manager still shepherded them around like a major impresario. The end of an unreal world.'

It was also the beginning of the end of touring to the Forces who were shortly to be demobbed in their millions. But there were still performances to be given for them, particularly at the isolated air stations — such as the strange night spent right at the end of Spurn Point in East Yorkshire where a small ack-ack unit was stationed under the command of two sergeants and where the Company stayed the night on the site of Smeaton's lighthouse. Leslie describes the atmosphere in some of the air stations:

'Audiences for Forces shows could vary from the enthusiastic to the solidly unresponsive. At one air-station during the plaster bombing of German cities air crews were ordered to attend a performance. All the members of the audience were kitted up in flying gear. They sat in grim silence like a mass of creatures from another planet. We might have been performing to Martians whose minds were preoccupied with other thoughts. At the end of the performance those acting were drained, exhausted and perplexed.

Very often we stayed in war-workers' hostels, army camps and air stations. In architectural aspect they were grim buildings, functional in concept, with a complete lack of charm. It was amazing how different the atmosphere could be in such similar establishments. Variously, too, we could be given hospitality with the officers, N.C.O.'s or "with other ranks". Some messes were warm and convivial, others grim and despairing. Sometimes we were honoured guests, at other times we could be treated impersonally.

At Wentworth Woodhouse, an army headquarters, I was accorded a batman in spite of explaining that a personal body servant was unnecessary. I explained my objection to the very intelligent elderly professional who was detailed, but "orders were orders" and my shoes were polished so brilliantly that I did not recognise them. At one air-station in remote Lincolnshire I remember news of the birth of a son coming to one of the officers in the midst of a convivial drinking session. "What is he going to be?" a jocular fellow asked the jubilant father. "I hope that he is going to be a conscientious objector," the airman replied, thoughtfully.

The most harrowing experience was being on an air-station during the raid on Dresden. The young pilots and air crew members were intelligent, well-educated people who knew exactly what they were ordered to do. They knew that Dresden was an historic and beautiful city and that it was an "Open City" full of refugees and practically defenceless. "We bombed it to hell," they said grimly. All agreed that the world had gone mad and we went for the whisky with suicidal abandon. Tables were stacked with bottles of Johnny Walker in a way that I have never seen before or since. We sang and joked with a forced cheerfulness as if there was no future.'

At around this time Wilfred Harrison, who had immensely strengthened the Company, intimated that he would need to leave as he was going to spend the next few years raising the thousands of pounds necessary to build John Ridley's amazing designs for a mobile theatre — The Century Theatre, of which, when completed, Wilfred was to be the director. Leslie Hardie also decided it was time to go. She explains why:

'War-time and the immediate post-war years were not pleasant in many ways. There was rationing, the black-out, an intolerable degree of compulsion for most people. As touring players we had an enviable degree of personal freedom and a varied and interesting life. At the same time, for me, it was a period of transition. The wandering life had no permanence, no possibility of a normal home life, a family life. There were social and sexual strains.

I left Compass Players at the end of 1946 at the end of a tour which finished with a week at the Library Theatre, Manchester. I had had a rough time with the manager who fought against our use of our own lighting. Previously we had given ten shows in eight different venues in one week. Notts and Derby Education Authority had diddled us out of payment for 20-odd school shows that we had already performed. I felt that, when educational authorities cut one short, England was an impossible place to succeed with our sort of theatre. Philistine beyond redemption. So I went to try my luck in Scandinavia.

I feel that we were fortunate and privileged to be Adelphi Players or Compass Players and I look back on the years with thankful appreciation.'

When Leslie returned from Scandinavia he spent some months helping to construct the Century Theatre and then worked as a relief worker in India and Pakistan as Head of a Society of Friends' Service Unit. He recently retired from the post of Senior Lecturer and Course Director at Bristol Polytechnic. John wrote in his memoirs: 'It is difficult to think how The Compass Players would have suvived its first years without all he had contributed.'

Other actors also left at this point and the Company was reduced to four players

— Anne and John Crockett, Paula Rice and Maurice Daniels. It was decided to set out in 1947 with these four plus a stage manager. A new repertoire had to be established.

So far the programmes that had been devised particularly for schools, audiences have not been mentioned. The first of these had been given the rather boring title XIVth to XIXth Century Drama, *and consisted of a mediaeval mystery play,* The Fall of Man, *a one act play by Hans Sachs,* The Strolling Clerk, *and a little ballet in the 18th-century mode danced to the entrancing music of Cimarosa, with Paula Rice as Columbine, Anne Crockett as Pantaloon and John Crockett as Harlequin. It was the success of this dance mime that led John to think further about creating his own productions that combined poetry, drama, music and dance as a whole, and in 1947 he began to develop his ideas for a schools' programme based on the story of the Fool in the theatre. During a long Christmas break he researched the topic in the British Museum Library and the London Library.*

The central idea was collected from a book by Enid Welsford called The Fool, his Social and Literary History (Faber 1935). *Other popular entertainments were researched including various versions of the mumming play as recorded all over the country, and the common elements of the struggle between a noble White Knight and a dark Black Knight and their revival by a magical Doctor were selected. For* 'underneath the near farcical was a deeply profound meaning,' *wrote John.* 'The mumming play was the vestige of a timeless universal myth that has persisted into the 20th century as I myself could vouch, having experienced it at the age of 13 while spending Christmas in a small Hampshire village and the local mummers burst into the house where I was staying, to perform their play.' *The compilation also included a Commedia dell' Arte scene and the company spent hilarious days improvising in true commedia style. To this was added a 17th-century jig* The Cheaters Cheated *which John had found in the London Library in a thesis on* The Elizabethan Jig and Related Song Drama *by Charles Read Baskerville (Chicago 1929). Then to the 18th century where a dance to Haydn's* Drum Roll *Symphony showing the development of the Commedia characters was followed by a Punch and Judy show where the actors performed as puppets. The illusion of puppets was achieved by masks with hoods that covered the whole head and shoulders. A dance, recreating the sad Pierrot of the 19th-century mime* Debureau, *was followed by on early 19th-century pantomime containing puns and jokes favoured by Grimaldi and ending with a chase between Clown, Harlequin and Columbine and a stolen string of sausages to the music of Offenbach's* Can Can. The Jester *was rehearsed during the winter of '46-'47 and John has described the problems they encountered:*

'That winter of '46-'47 was one of the cruellest in living memory and the country, still rationed and weary from the years of war, more or less came to a halt under a cruel blanket of snow. The Warren, rather remote, situated near the top of a long hill and with a drive about half a mile long that was like a switchback, became isolated. The wonderful village grocer, Mr Jones, from Aylburton, about three miles away, managed to get his little van to the gates of the drive with provisions, but from there everything had to be taken by sledge. To keep warm, before rehearsals started every morning everyone had to don whatever warm clothing they possessed and rubber boots and go out into the woods armed with axes and saws and cut down trees that in turn had to be sawn into logs. The electric light for the estate derived from the ancient Lister engine which had a habit of failing without warning. But despite this rehearsals went quite merrily.'

What a delightful show it must have been and enormously successful with schools and audiences all over the country. The Company felt bitter, however, when another company, working solely in the field of children's theatre, took the idea and presented it as their own. Something one has to learn in the theatre — there is no copyright on ideas! But it was particularly galling as this theatre company was the only one to retain its grants when the cuts to mobile touring were made in the late 1940s, although The Compass Players never received subsidy from the Arts Council anyway — there were always too many strings attached.

A play by Richard Ward called Of Gods and Men *was the next production. It moved swiftly from the world of ancient Greek myth to England in the 1940s. Each of the four actors had to play many parts. The opening scene was of Zeus on the phone to his wife, making excuses for his dalliances with lesser goddesses. John Crockett played Zeus and also had to be Aidoneus, King of Hell, and in the 20th century a fraudulent medium pretending to be an Italian, and another part of a rather specious clergyman. Anne Crockett recalls the dancing in these plays:*

'Many of our programmes, such as the story of the Fool through the ages called *The Jester*, had as much dancing and miming as speech, but even for those plays that had no actual dancing I insisted on the Company doing dance drama technical exercises and lyrical movements daily. These were based on breath control. Drawing in the breath and holding it gave the accent and tension, breathing out gave relaxation, and the "following through" and completion of a movement. Doing these exercises greatly improved an actor or actress's timing, which is vitally important in acting and makes speech rhythmical and accented in the right places; it gives meaning to a phrase, as in music the placing of the climax (the most important accent) gives shape to a musical phrase. We were fortunate to have Paula Rice as one of our first members. She had trained at the Ginner Mawer School and was a lovely dancer. She made a beautiful Persephone in Richard Ward's *Of Gods and Men*. The theme of the play dealt with the rape of Persephone by Pluto, and scenes of Olympus were juxtaposed with scenes of modern life.

For the scene where she is picking flowers before Pluto snatches her into the Underworld we used *Venus* from Holst's *Planet Suite*. We used pieces from the other Planets for different scenes; *Mars* for the King of the Underworld; *Jupiter* for the Overture and for Zeus' appearances; *Uranus* for the mysterious scenes and *Mercury* for the Messenger scenes. They fitted very well, and I cannot now hear any of the Planet music without seeing scenes from the play in my mind's eye.'

Whilst touring in Kent, Charles Landstone, the deputy director of drama for the newly formed Arts Council of Great Britian, visited a performance of Of Gods and Men, *and is reported to have said: "Well, I take off my hat to The Compass Players for having the courage to put on this play so well but heaven knows what it's all about." The Arts Council tours to the theatreless towns had resumed in the spring of 1947 after a break in funding but this was to last for only a short time and they preferred to promote their own tours rather than provide subsidy for already established theatre groups. What they failed to appreciate then (and even now) was that if an idealistic company tries to fit in with Arts Council policies it can restrict its freedom of artistic expression.*

The next new play written for the company was a version of Chaucer's Pardoner's Tale *in an adaptation by John Crockett with a longer version called* The Last Enemy. *It was very popular and contained some quite complex dancing to Stravinsky's* Firebird *and* Sacré du Printemps.

But the strong nucleus of the Company was about to be broken up. Paula Rice, who had been with the Company almost since its beginning, decided to leave. She too has recalled those years for us:

'We were able to perform on any type of platform, large or small, or even on the floor in the midst of people. Having screens as a background rather than scenery meant that we could expand or contract our background and make entrances and exits by careful placing of screens wherever we wanted them. The props and the costumes were cleverly designed by John and made by all and sundry. They gave a sense of colour and period to the plays, and lighting and music set the atmosphere. Leslie was the Stage Manager and he carried out the Producer's lighting demands in a most heroic way. I have seen him scale steel girders in aerodrome hangars and fix lights to them. He did the same from the rafters of churches. Once, he carried out John's idea of spot-lighting the fascinating carvings in an old church, which were so hidden in dark corners that the local audience beheld them for the first time. It was wonderful how village halls and school hall platforms with no theatrical atmosphere were brought to life by the clever placing of lights! And he was a wizard with curtains: if there were any when we arrived he often had to mend the arrangement for drawing them. I only remember a curtain getting stuck once in all the time I was with the Company - a good record I think!

An important factor, which made us available even to the smallest community, was the small fee we asked. We needed very little money for ourselves. Most of what we got went back to produce further plays and to support us during rehearsal times. I believe we might have asked about £12 to start with. At one point, I remember, it was £15. However, in the case of churches we probably just accepted the collection, and we were very grateful for food and a night's shelter. I never dealt with finances: this is simply what I gathered from listening to financial discussions. None of us received wages. Those who needed comforts such as cigs or sweets were given the money, and no-one protested. We also received money for sheer necessities, but big items such as coats or shoes were really thought about, and, if necessary, a Company meeting was called. No-one got clothes if it was thought that his or her present garments could go on for a little longer. There was no concern about how we looked off-stage; after all, whatever we wore was always crushed and crumpled looking!

I remember that it was fairly difficult to find suitable places to wash our hair when on tour, and it got so greasy with the make-up. I once plucked up my courage to ask my hostess if I could possibly wash my hair in her sink (that was the only place in which washing seemed to be done in her house). She allowed me to do so, but asked in a very disapproving way if I was Welsh. When I said, "No," she said, "Oh I thought you were: I so dislike the Welsh!" But she was an exception; nearly always people opened their homes to us, and put us to bed with warm drinks and sent us off in the mornings with good breakfasts. Such generosity was specially kind when one remembers how strict the food-rationing was. Often, the local Women's Institute gave us an evening meal. In Scotland, we just could not get over the variety of bread, buns and scones and jam we were given.

First contacts, to introduce our company and then to make bookings for us, were the responsibility of one or sometimes two people going ahead. The usual procedure was to interest someone in the community who would undertake to raise the fee by selling tickets or by group collection, and to see that our posters were displayed and accommodation arranged. These agents for our company were usually very young women and they did wonderful work. I can only remember one occasion of failure of our bookings, when we had to split up for about six weeks. Those of us who felt we would be able to get work and support ourselves for that short time did so. I suppose some might have spent the time with relatives, but anyone at a loss was able to go back to our home base, a beautiful old house in Gloucestershire, set in extensive grounds on which there was a farmhouse, used by a religious, farming and potters' community and, as John and the man who inspired this settled community had a long-standing friendship (this man's name was George Ineson), our two very different types of community mixed whenever possible and had a mutually beneficial influence on one another. We would go to them full of things to tell them about our travels, and they could show us their growth, brought about by steady application and devotion to place. They built a chapel. They tilled the fields and made pottery. Men and women interchanged jobs quite a bit, but, even if this idea was not very developed, the women took it in turns to look after the children so that some were always free to go into the fields.

I remember that we had the good luck to share with them the celebration of one of their Harvest Homes. The table was spread down the length of the whole room and we sat on benches, filling the room with young children, young parents and young people generally; everything on the table was home-grown and home-cooked and a spirit of joy was in all of us. Strange to think now, when at that time so much death and destruction was going on, how the wonderful old celebration still gave all present such unity and unmixed happiness.

These houses and the land were lent to the two communities, which otherwise could not have developed. It was a real joy to return to our headquarters: it was a home to us. Anne always became the Goddess of the Hearth when we returned, and it was her love of the house and grounds that helped to make it such a special place. She always got the Aga going as soon as possible and in no time had something good cooking on it and in it! She soon managed to have stores of food in the larder. The kitchen was always spotless and the day after our arrival she would admonish us, male and female alike, to polish the wooden floors, stairs and bannisters with the O-Cedar oil which she always had handy in a large can, pervading the house with the scent of cedar trees. Wood from the grounds made the huge evening fires which we all enjoyed. The hearth was very large, in a large hall, and we sat round with warmth and comfort and time to relax. Anne would sometimes plant vegetables and flowers when we were rehearsing, so we came home to vegetables and flowers and eggs from the farm, and I suppose milk as well, at any rate we always had it.

Another great benefit for us all was the ability to wander off on our own between rehearsals. We needed these breaks from one another because normally our lives were lived in such a tightknit community. We were lucky to get plenty of time for our rehearsals: it gave us a margin for renewal and creative growth.

Apart from acting, everyone else had something to be responsible for. I had to write ahead to the organisers to ask whether any people in the community could put us up, or whether we needed to find alternative accommodation. It was very rare indeed for us to have to go to a hotel; if we did we could never afford more than the type of hotel used by commercial travellers. If we were really stuck we used Youth Hostels if there were any in the area. I remember when once in Edinburgh we were staying in a Youth Hostel I felt ill; it was probably 'flu. We all had to get up early (no lying in bed in Youth Hostels), fold our blankets neatly and do some work around the hostel before leaving. The others must have done my work for me as I was in a daze, and directly I could leave I flopped down on the nearest bit of grass and stayed there all day. It seemed to me as I drowsed that it must have been a bit of grass entirely surrounded by traffic, as I seemed continually to hear vehicles going by. One or other of the Company took it in turn to sit by me. In the evening we made our way to the theatre and there the old magic worked once again and, as I began to make up, the illness gradually retreated and, once launched into the play, it had gone completely. I suppose it returned afterwards, but I was over the worst; I think most of us must have reacted in that way, for none of us ever had time off on grounds of illness.

The Hostel was a great standby. The snag was that no-one could get into the Hostel unless they arrived on foot or by bicycle, so we had to hide our van and hide our occupation. We also had to arrive at an early hour, which made it difficult when doing evening performances. I think though that we probably used these hostels most often between bookings. We also stayed in Army and Navy barracks. It was then that we were able to get baths and hot water, so that we all set to to help Anne wash the wardrobe, but how she dried all those costumes I never found out.

When we entered any of the Forces' camps we were issued with passes. Once I lost mine and, as we were only staying there for the evening performance, there was no time to get another issued, so I was accompanied everywhere by two soldiers! Backwards and forwards from dressing room to stage and even to the toilet!! When the Americans finally arrived, the contrast between the food we were kindly offered after our performance and the fare offered by the other Forces was amazing. To start with, it was the first time any of us had been introduced to hamburgers, but the huge tins of fruit and literally buckets of ice cream just left us gasping.

The saddest times I always felt were going into the Air Force messes after our performances. Here we met men whose nerves were stretched to breaking-point; they drank steadily, and they created their own jargon, which helped them verbally to skid over the continuous loss of companions, and the knowledge that each flight they made lessened their chances of survival. It was because there were so few of them as compared to the other Forces, and they all knew each other so well.

Once we played to a Polish camp,, and afterwards the men begged us girls to dance. Heavens! There were so few of us and so many of them, we never stopped whirling for hours it seemed, and we were taught Polish dances; it certainly was an extraordinarily lively evening. Sometimes we were put up for the night, or even several nights, by rich and privileged people in big houses; they were always kind and polite but I was never really at ease in those places.

Finally I left the Company. It was a sad parting on both sides. They gave me all they could spare at the time, which was £5. Enough to last a careful person about two weeks. I headed for London because I thought I would try my luck in the theatre there, and also I knew I could soon get jobs as a model to tide me over. I hitched up so as not to break into the money. I was so lucky: two brothers picked me up and, when they heard my tale and the hopes I had of a new start, they dropped me at Camden Town and called me over to say goodbye. One of them handed me something and said: "Good luck! We were just like you a few years ago," and drove off. When I opened my hand there was £5!! So now I had four weeks in which to find my feet!

What a happy beginning to my new life...'

Paula never returned to the theatre. She worked as an artists' model and raised her family. She then retired to a Welsh village where for the first time since the Compass days she produced some plays in the village church.

Anne Crockett also felt the need for a more settled existence and explains some of the changes that occurred at this point in the Compass history:

John was an artist and had an artist's capacity for taking pains. He put as much creative energy into directing the Company as he did into his paintings, and his artist's insistence on getting things right, as perfect as possible, was an inspiration. We all helped and shared all tasks, but John designed all the costumes and sets, and the publicity (posters and handbills and the programmes). We were lucky in that Connie Ineson was a professional dressmaker and could make the costumes from John's designs so we did not have to sew them from the beginning, but everybody trimmed and decorated and sewed on buttons and bows, and made props.

When we had finished a production, after the First Night, John became a professional photographer. His photographs of the cast, as if in action, were excellent and made good publicity photographs. My memories of rehearsal were of John working away at one thing after another and never stopping. One typical scene stays in my memory: I was doing dance exercises in one room with a group and John had emerged from the adjoining room where he was rehearsing a scene with another group. As he waited for the next scene to be "set" he was weeding the garden, so as not to waste time. I called him to come and help me by showing my group some leg swings, a manoeuvre he with his very long legs was well equipped to do. After dancing up and down the room, showing off his high kicks and while we flopped down breathless on the floor to rest, he went straight back to his weeding. He never rested.

But I was approaching the ripe age of 30 and I longed for a baby and a settled home with no travelling, though I had enjoyed the travelling through the countryside. The roads at the end of the war were beautifully empty so that the scenery could be enjoyed more easily than it can be today. But after eight years of marriage I felt it was time to have a family. The urge became irresistible when my younger sister, also a member of a travelling theatrical company, the Adelphi Players, gave up touring and acting to produce her first child. John was persuaded to stop touring also because he wanted to return to his painting. For the last five years he had had no time at all for this and he felt he had been long enough away from it. I had loved acting and felt very sad every time the company left The Warren, our rehearsal centre, but I loved babies more, and The Warren began to live up to its name as John and I went on to produce eight of them (not all at once, but through the next thirteen years). I never acted again, though I did some school teaching, which I suppose was the next best thing.'

Maurice Daniels now became the Company Manager when The Compass Players were on tour and Anne and John Crockett remained at The Warren. John was painting a great deal and he and Anne awaited the birth of their first child.

New actors were about to join the Company. They were among the first of the new post-war generation and had something of the passionate idealism of those days. They will now continue the story taking, as their individual themes, the area of the Company's work for which they held special responsibility in addition to acting. Their recollections of those years will include the final break up of the Company and their own evaluation of the experience of being a Compass Player and its effect on their subsequent careers, for some in teaching drama and for others in acting and working in the theatre. They tell too of their emotional and spiritual growth and understanding during those intense years from 1948-52. and of how they came to be called The Compass Magicians.

PART TWO

1948 — 1952

I

BEGINNINGS AND CONNECTIONS

Pamela Dellar

The train pulled out of Blakeney station and gradually gained speed, puffing along by the banks of the River Severn through some of the loveliest of England's countryside, lush and leafy in the height of that summer of 1948. 'Next stop Lydney,' the guard had shouted and nervously I started to tidy myself up in preparation for the audition ordeal to come. Not that I was unused to auditions. I'd done several that summer after my drama school's final public show which was held at the Globe Theatre in Shaftesbury Avenue and where all the agents came looking for talent.

Those of us who weren't chosen as Rank starlets, and this was the majority, trotted round the London agents trying to convince them that the theatre needed us. One thing I learned quickly was that, in order to get oneself noticed, an introduction from someone else helped. I was lucky. A family friend took an interest in my ambitions. Andrew MacLaren had been Labour M.P. for Stoke and he used his influence to get me an interview with C.B.Cochran, the famous impresario whose 'young ladies' had been immensely popular during the war years. Cochran was now an old man, shrinking into the cracked leather of his office armchair and after talking to me (I really wasn't his type and was not trained in musical theatre anyway) he gave me a further introduction to a young agent called Phil Brown who actually took me on to his books. I had also expressed enthusiasm for the Irish theatre and Andrew MacLaren obtained an interview for me with Lord Longford. I recall travelling across the thick green carpet of his Piccadilly office and nervously quaking at his large desk. He took my hand and, after holding it quite warmly for a little while, gave me an introduction to go to Ireland to be auditioned by Hilton Edwards and Micheál

'John had to go to Gloucester so he can't audition you today,' said Penny. 'The rest of us are helping to get the corn in. Would you like...?' She broke off with a look at my sartorial elegance. I almost wept with dismay.

'I could lend you some dungarees,' she said, hesitantly. I accepted, and a few minutes later, attired in a pair of landgirl's dungarees and wellingtons a couple of sizes too big, was hurrying down to the field. What a blissful summer afternoon that was, gathering in the sheaves of barley when the tractor had cut it, tying it into bundles and then placing the bundles in stooks to dry out. Finally the rabbits all made a run for it as the tractor trundled up to cut the last few yards and the field was finished. The Taena people wandered off to their farm and to their secret and enviable close-knit community life and we went back up to the Warren for an evening meal.

The next morning I was auditioned. My pieces were — Deidre in *Deidre of the Sorrows* by J.M.Synge. 'Draw a little back with the squabbling of fools when I'm broken up with misery.' Strong western Irish accent which I felt I had perfected on my visit to Dublin! This I followed with the tea party scene from *The Importance of Being Earnest.* I played both Cecily and Gwendolin! And finally a piece from a West End success of the '40s by Robert Morley called *Goodness How Sad!* As students we had taken it to Holloway jail where our captive audience had been particularly enthusiastic about our handsome and virile young actors.

At the end of the audition, which was solely for John Crockett, he raised himself wearily from a chair, shuffled some papers, went out to the loo, came back, moved a chair and a typewriter, swore mildly about his wife, his colleagues and the problems of running a theatre company and then said, yes, he thought I'd be suitable to play the parts they were casting at the moment, after which he muttered something about 'coffee time' and disappeared again like the White Rabbit. I saw him next through an open door in the studio with paints and brushes, working on a painting.

The house was full of John's paintings. Two remain vividly in my memory. One hung over the fireplace in the hall. It was of Adam and Eve encircling a child in the embryo, inspired by John and Anne's first child who had been born that summer. Another, hanging at the foot of the stairs, was of a drowing man — the head and hands disappearing in the swirling sea.

But now, at last, I was to be a fully professional actress. I was to be paid 15/- per week and all found. The 'all found' even included necessary clothing and toiletries. I left on top of the world.

When I got home there was a telephone call from the agent Phil Brown offering me a part in a number one tour of *Charley's Aunt* and another call from a television producer. Ungraciously I turned them down flat. I felt I would learn more working with a company like The Compass Players. One of those life decisions that at the time seem simple and yet turn out to be of life-long importance.

We went into rehearsal two weeks later. Of the plays we were to work on two were already in the repertoire. *The Last Enemy* was an adaptation by John Crockett of Chaucer's *Pardoner's Tale,* and I was replacing an actress who had left. The other was *The Man of Destiny* by George Bernard Shaw and I was to prompt and stage manage.

The Last Enemy was a unique mixture of dance, music, masks, lighting and colourful costume. My drama school training had provided little to prepare me for this type of theatrical presentation. The dialogue was simple enough but the dance and movement were quite extraordinary. Anne trained us for this every evening after supper when the baby was tucked up for the night. I had done Greek dancing from the age of three and I loved it. The style that Anne taught us was also barefooted but whereas the Greek dancing was concerned with line and form, based on the figures on Greek vases, this new dance was based on impulse from the centre of the body and breathing. On the breath in, the body movement expands, and, on breathing out, contracts. One movement sequence in particular seemed to provide total body release and formed a basis for the choreography. It was called the 'ripple through'. The body dropped loosely forward, knees were pushed forward, then hips, shoulders, head, as the hands pushed upwards to the sky. It was a whiplash movement through the whole body and could push in any direction.

What we were being taught of course were the early techniques which Martha Graham had developed in the U.S.A. during the '20s and '30s. Anne had learnt them from Margaret Barr, a former pupil of Graham. Even so, Anne herself was a superb teacher and brought something of her own to each dance session. We were privileged to receive this training long before the London School of Contemporary Dance brought Graham's methods to the forefront of dance training in this country. I went to see Graham and her company when they visited London for the first time in the early 1950s and I was amazed that I could recognise the movement sequences and style in her remarkable ballets.

The music we were using in *The last Enemy* was Stravinsky's *Firebird* and *The Rite of Spring* (this was 1948 remember and Stravinsky was still an acquired taste). I can recall the counting for the dance of the houris in the brothel scene. This was to *Firebird* and went 1 - 2 - 3 - 4 - 5 - 6 - 7 - 8 and point; and point; 1 - 2 - 3 - 4 - 5 - 6 - 7 - 8 and point; ripple through. Very staccato sequence followed by a short extended passage.

These dance and movement sessions did more for us than just help us to dance in a play. They were partly responsible for our company style which made us different from other theatre companies at the time and from our 'family' companies like the Adelphis and later the Century Theatre. Also they provided a release for the whole person. On one occasion when we were training for *Dr Faustus,* I remember staying in the rehearsal room and dancing to Richard Strauss's *Heldenleben.* For the first time in my life I experienced the total freedom of being able to dance. I used to get up early in the morning before anyone else was awake and run and dance down the long drive. I must have looked strange in my youthful enthusiasm for the dance as Richard Ward hastened to point out on one occasion when he was visiting us. But dance, almost as much as music, can provide emotional release. When a person is anguished the body needs to move. People 'race up and down' or 'thrash from side to side' or 'rock backwards and forwards' to release their pain. One becomes 'unbalanced' or 'on edge' or doesn't know 'which way to turn'. If one can dance it is possible to impose a control over this restlessness by creating formal patterns of movement to express the trapped emotions. At times of intense sadness I have found that dancing can provide true solace and I learnt to appreciate the therapeutic nature of dance as well as the artistic purpose during those Compass years.

But now, suddenly, there was a great flurry of preparation. The O'Cedar furniture polish appeared and feverish cleaning, dusting and polishing began. Anne and John moved out of their room and it was prepared for the important guests who were to arrive shortly to start work on the final production to complete the autumn repertoire. Maurice Browne was coming to direct *Dr Knock* by Jules Romains.

Maurice was old and ill. Shrivelled up and constantly munching charcoal biscuits as if to fuel his remaining sparks of energy, he was cosseted by his 'adopted daughter', Molly Underwood, who even took over rehearsals for him at times. But he was treated with great respect. It was only in later years that I understood how important his own wrecked idealism had been to Adelphis and Compasses, and how his methods had influenced the work of R. H. Ward and John Crockett.

Maurice Browne had been a great impresario. He brought Paul Robeson to London in *Othello* and produced *Journey's End* in London in the 1920's. In his biography *Too Late to Lament* he speaks of how, in later life, he made many productions for two groups of young people with high ideals, the Adelphi and The Compass Players. 'I felt deeply grateful for the opportunity to expiate in part the betrayal of a dream, dreamed three decades before in Chicago,' he said. It was in Chicago, in the second decade of the century, that Maurice Browne and his American wife, Ellen van Volkenburg, developed an exciting, idealistic and community-centred theatre company that is credited with being the founder of the American Little Theatre movement.

The writer, John Cowper Powys, who became a close friend of Browne, reviewed their production of *The Trojan Women* with sonorous enthusiasm: 'For the directors of the Chicago Little Theatre the whole world resolves itself into an Act of Worship...the voice of the Unknown World-Priest intoning through the ages, and the voice of innumerable generations answering.'

This intense theatrical idealism must have fragmented and permeated many subsequent theatrical enterprises. Once enmeshed in it, one finds it impossible to escape and I have found myself trapped with this vision of the power of theatre throughout my life. Perhaps I should trace it back to Maurice Browne and Nelly van. Theirs was a total theatre of music, dance, mask and puppetry. Their god was Gordon Craig. Dorothy and Leonard Elmhurst of Dartington recognised Maurice's particular genius and bought a cottage for him to live in in his declining years with Molly, which is where he came from to direct for the Compasses at The Warren. But his energy had faded and I can only recall one rehearsal when, having reduced me to tears, which was not difficult, he came out of the rehearsal room saying that I did have a glimmer of talent as an actress. Praise indeed!

I was having problems with my acting but found Stanislavsky's *An Actor Prepares* a great help and I also used to write meticulously in the column of my play copy exactly what I was thinking when other people were talking. This was because of John's emphasis on learning how to listen on the stage. Before long I was able to give up this arduous task.

As far as I know *Dr Knock* was Maurice's last production for Adelphis and Compasses. He died in 1955 and J.C.Powys wrote to his friend Louis Wilkinson: 'The Maurice I knew when I first met him, and perhaps the later Maurice too, were different from the Maurice of the Little Theatre time. The Maurice of the Little Theatre was a maniacal Messiah of theatrical art.' (Letter to Louis Wilkinson: Macdonald and Co., 1958) So the unresolved question remains — was the dying spark still there amongst the charcoal biscuits? Probably not, but I am convinced that it was there within the infectious and sometimes arrogant ideals of The Compass Players.

On the hill by The Warren there were bushes and a summer house left over from a more affluent period. Frequently we would see George Ineson appear from the hillside. He was concerned with Buddhist philosophy at that time and I think he used to meditate looking out over the beautiful view of the Severn. I was rather in awe of George. He had a very soulful face, full of suffering, and I always felt that he was deeply involved in solving the nature of the universe. I was shy of speaking to him in case I disturbed him just as he was discovering a great universal truth.

The actor who was playing Dr Knock was sleeping in the summer house and one day he didn't turn up for the morning rehearsal. I went to see what the matter was and he said he wasn't coming out. When I went again he said he would like some dinner. I went to the kitchen where Anne was feeding the baby. 'Tell him if he wants it to come and get it,' said Anne grimly. John picked up an earthenware bowl of bread and butter pudding and went out to the summer house. He returned with the look of a dejected spaniel. 'I've told him to go. I shall have to play Knock.' It was a great disappointment to John as he had hoped for a season at home with Anne and the baby, doing some painting. He had to rehearse very quickly and he wasn't a brilliant actor at the best of times.

So we set off on the autumn tour. Maurice Daniels, the company manager, driving. Maurice was slimly built, very amusing and a splendid character actor; then there was Moira Deady, a brilliant Irish actress, now a star of television in Ireland; Hedley Lunn, an ex-Adelphi player, devoted to Moira and a very serious and skilful actor. He played Napoleon in Shaw's *The Man of Destiny*. Later he developed an illness and gave up the theatre entirely. There were also two raw actors, like me, just out of Central School. One was Martin Heller who stayed with Compasses to the end and the other was Dorothy Grumbar who only stayed till Christmas.

The tour remains only vaguely in the memory. We opened at a huge theatre at Grange over Sands in North Lancashire — my first professional performance. I recall a performance at Clitheroe and being severely berated by John for leaving holes in his tights (I had also taken on the job of wardrobe mistress — a task for which I am totally unsuited as I have five thumbs on each hand). The most eventful thing was when Grumbar (I always called her Grumbar, never Dorothy, an old Central School habit; for some reason we always used surnames there) was leaving and I wrote to my friend Armine Sandford to see if she'd like to apply for the job. She was appearing in twice nightly weekly rep in Blackburn and wrote back swiftly to say yes. The thought of long rehearsal periods was a great attraction in those days where weekly rep was the norm. John interviewed her after seeing her perform in *The Rotters* and she joined us in January 1949.

Armine and I had met at the Central School during the first term of our training. We were both standing at the noticeboard looking for lodgings. Armine reminds me that I was wearing my emerald green slacks and she turned to me and said, 'Would you like to share a room in the hostel?' I remember noticing her brilliant red hair and saying, 'Yes', and that was that. We shared for the rest of our time at drama school — first in the hostel in Kensington High Street, and then in a flat in Nevern Square, Earls Court, which we shared with a theatrical agent who specialised in variety acts. Both of these were convenient for the school, which was situated in the Albert Hall! For there, behind the grandeur of the huge auditorium, there lies a maze of smaller rooms, a labyrinth in fact which housed studios, offices and a little theatre. We used to creep into the hall and watch famous conductors, such as Richard Strauss, rehearsing, or the Women's Institute rallies singing *Jerusalem*, or the latest boxing tournament with Sugar Ray Robinson.

Armine and I got on very well and still remain good friends. When we worked with Compasses we complemented each other. Armine played 'upstairs' characters like Dynamene in *A Phoenix Too Frequent* and I played the maid, Doto. She played Celimene in *Le Misanthrope* and I played Eliante. Altogether we studied, lived, worked and even took holidays together for about seven years at Central School and Compasses and Century Theatre.

'You see the country at any rate,' was the familiar phrase that greeted us as we travelled round with The Compass Players and this was true, even though it was often but a fleeting moment. Mostly we received hospitality from our audience and this provided us with a unique insight into social class, and taught us to accept whatever bed was provided. For instance, we slept in individual four-poster beds at Ormesby Hall in Middlesborough as the guests of Colonel and Mrs Pennyman and then the following night found ourselves offered a double bed in a two-up, two-down in Washington, County Durham.

The Pennymans had always supported theatre companies and for a while had housed Joan Littlewood and Ewan MacColl and the famous Theatre Workshop. There was a time when they offered a permanent base to the Compasses and John travelled up from Gloucestershire to discuss it with them. But when it came to the decision he found it impossible to break away from Taena and the Community and there was agreement that such a move would have broken the magic of The Warren and all it stood for.

But it was lovely staying at Ormesby and to be greeted by Colonel Pennyman's cry at breakfast time of, 'Anyone want the dessicated cardboard?', and then for us girls to be taken round the grounds and given his lecture on forestry! Once, when they were away they still let us stay there and, as accommodation officer, I felt very grand discussing the meals with cook, although actually she just said what she thought and I agreed.

There was another time when it was suggested that we settle elsewhere. John was summoned to London for 'discussions' with Michael MacOwan and Charles Landstone of the Arts Council. They had the bright idea that Compasses should settle in Gainsborough — an area with which we had absolutely no affiliations — and that the first production should be *Arms and the Man*. John has written, 'In other words the company was being offered a certain amount of financial aid at the cost of becoming little more than a slightly classy rep, performing plays that were already popular and forsaking all theatrical experiment and innovation. The two men were quite surprised when I turned the proposal down flat!' The story has a ring of familiarity for many present day companies who have preferred to follow their own policies rather than those of the arts administrators. (7.84 Theatre Company? Mediaeval Players?)

It is mildly interesting to find that Charles Landstone, in his book, *Off Stage*, makes only brief mention of the Adelphi companies and none of The Compass Players. Yet C.E.M.A. (later the Arts Council) did fund the Adelphis, and all the companies did provide a classical repertoire second to none. Compasses presented Shaw, Molière, Fry, Marlowe, Tchekov and Milton, as well as new plays with dance and masks. But then, his book, which records the first twelve years of state sponsored drama in Great Britain 1939-51, does not mention Joan Littlewood or Theatre Workshop either. Travelling theatre was pretty low on the Arts Council list of priorities in the late 1940's as at that time they were trying to establish regional centres.

I was reading avidly at this time. I read anything that anyone recommended and it was rather a heady mixture. Maurice suggested *The Magic Mountain* by Thomas Mann. The influence of Tacna led to my reading *The Spirit of Chinese Philosophy* and a fascinating book by John Layard called *The Lady and the Hare* which was concerned with Jungian interpretation of dreams. Then of course I read D.H.Lawrence and John Cowper Powys. I later discovered that R.H.Ward had written a book about the Powys brothers in about 1935 and that J.C.Powys had referred to him as 'this gnomic and enigmatic young man, belonging to the good "Left" of our obscure New Generation.' (Letter to Louis Wilkinson.) The Richard we knew was still enigmatic if no longer young. He was the intellectual force behind the Adelphi, Compass and early Century theatres and his lengthy correspondence with John Crockett shows his deep commitment to the ideals of cultural democracy.

As we travelled great distances in the van we would sleep, talk, discuss, argue, read and sing. Some of us loved harmonizing and Hedley Lunn gave a splendid rendition of the Peter Pears favourite *The Foggy-Foggy Dew*, and I offered my version of Kathleen Ferrier's *Blow the Wind Southerly*. On one journey a huge white owl flew into the side of the van and we speculated as to whether it was 'a baker's daughter' *(Hamlet)*. Once a man, walking down the street, turned to look at the van and walked straight into a lamppost — truly!

Our discussions in the back of the van were about our acting. Whether to go for a single big laugh instead of two small laughs; whether a pause before a word would help to get a laugh; whether a turn upstage was killing another actor's line. Problems of technique, style and team playing.

Maurice, who was company manager, maintained a strict discipline. We did not dare to be late. If the van was to move off at 9.30 a.m. we were there. I always date my obsession with punctuality from those days. Maurice was also very aware of the importance of public relations. 'Pam,' he would say as we crossed the border into Wales, 'when we get there on no account must you leap out of the van speaking with a Welsh accent!' Similarly in Devon, Somerset, Lancashire and particularly in Scotland. It was a unique opportunity to brush up on my regional accents.

Occasionally we gave a free performance in exchange for overnight accommodation. This included prisons. We played at an open prison in Sudbury, Derbyshire. There was an unusual audience response to Shaw's *The Man of Destiny*. Great cheers rang out whenever Napoleon showed any physical aggression towards the Lady. We women slept that night in the prison hospital, where the assistant cook, an old lag, brought us our early morning cup of tea.

We were in Matlock during the winter, climbing up the steep hill to our digs in pouring rain and deserted streets, when a policeman stopped us. 'Where do you think you're going?' he said. 'You look as if you've just come out of the Ark.' Admittedly, we were in strange clothing. Johnny Ringham was wearing his duffle coat with the hood up, I was wearing my baggy dark brown corduroy trousers with ankle length coat to match, and Armine wore a voluminous macintosh and carried a capacious handbag. It was difficult to look respectable when we were living out of small suitcases and only staying one night in the same place.

Luckily we stayed with some of the nicest people in the country. During the war small towns and villages had set up organisations to promote the arts and these organisations still gave us hospitality. We had to give them our rations and would turn up late at night with a tiny portion of butter, a screw of tea and another of sugar. Things were getting easier now, so often our meagre contributions were not accepted. Sometimes we were given a meal with members of the audience between matinees and evening performances and it was at Bishop Auckland I recall an earnest school teacher turning to me and saying, 'Have you seen Donald Wolfit's Bottom?' My reply was a somewhat strangulated negative!

Often our hosts would say, 'We used to have the Arts League of Service — now they were really marvellous'. Who were these people? What were their plays like? The replies were rather vague. Then in 1974 I came across a book in a Hay-on-Wye bookshop. It was called *Travelling Players* and was a history of the Arts League of Service written by their director, Eleonor Elder. In it she tells how she had returned from India, just before the end of the First World War, eager to establish a travelling theatre which aimed 'to bring the Arts into Everyday Life'. She had trained in Frank Benson's Shakespearian Company and these earlier contacts helped her to found her own company in 1919. They performed mainly short one-act plays, some specially written for them by famous writers such as James Stephens, Gordon Bottomley, A.J. Talbot, F. Sladen-Smith, and original work such as *Hagoromo*, translated by Ezra Pound with music by Edmund Rubbra. Actors of calibre worked with them including Donald Wolfit, Sara Allgood, Alan Wheatley, Andrew Cruikshank, Angela and Hermione Baddeley, and the dancer Margaret Barr had choreographed for them. They travelled the length and breadth of Britain and on one occasion played before the King and Queen at Balmoral. They played at Settle, Clitheroe, Alrincham, Marple, Ilkley, Keighley and when The Compass Players visited these places, twelve years after the A.L.S. had disbanded in 1937, and with the war between us, we found the audiences still remembered them and we ouselves benefited from their pioneering work.

The long tours were immensely tiring and it was always a relief to return to The Warren and to Anne's warm welcome, ready to start on another production and rehearsal period. One summer a lively dark-haired Welsh girl joined us as a general dogsbody and skivvy. She had immense vitality and threw herself into cleaning floors and cooking meals with the dynamic energy she applied to everything she did. Her name was Rachel Roberts and she later became famous as a stage and film actress and wife of Rex Harrison. Rachel did not stay long. One day she told me that a very important and famous director had asked her to go to Paris with him and she had decided to go. I did not really believe her at first but the next day she left. She was too much of an individualist ever to become a Compass Player but she was very stimulating and I did enjoy her company very much.

And so the long summer rehearsal period went on — rehearsals, dance classes, learning lines. I look back now and see Armine and Connie Ineson bent over the sewing machines till the early hours of the morning creating 17th-century costumes from John's designs, and John working in the outhouse, building up the meticulously constructed papier maché masks. I see myself in the old scullery, with the primus stove and pan of boiling water full of purple dye for dyeing the hessian curtains on which John will shortly stencil an elaborate pattern. Maurice toiling till all hours in the office confirming the bookings. Joyce and Anne cooking a delicious meal in the kitchen and feeding babies. Johnny Ringham labouring over the van at the bottom of the steps outside and Martin battling with the switchboard in the rehearsal room. Not for us a night at the pub or the pictures. Not for us a shopping trip to town. We worked on some of the greatest plays in the English language, we thrilled to the poetry of Marlowe, Milton, Synge and Shaw. We enjoyed each other's company, we ate good food, we breathed fresh unpolluted air, we were totally immersed in our work and pattern of living.

Such close relationships inevitably led to emotional attachments and sometimes these were unhappy ones. John Crockett described in his memoirs how *The Last Enemy* (1947) was written 'at a time of great distress for the playwright', and our understanding of a series of paintings he painted around that time is, I think, increased by the recognition of their emotional content. They are some of his best paintings and include a series of Pierrot, Harlequin and Columbine; then *The Creation* and the slightly later picture which he described as a self-portrait and is entitled *Supplicating Man Drowning in Shallow Water*.

In the spring of 1950 we were in Newton Stewart in Galloway. We had a few days without bookings and John and I went for a walk through the spectacular countryside catching occasional glimpses of fleeting deer as we passed near the forest. During the walk John explained to me some of the emotional and marital problems that existed for him in the company, and over the next 18 months we developed a close relationship which later became a life-long friendship. But in the summer of 1951 a crisis point was reached which affected us all. The crisis was precipitated by my parents discovering the nature of our relationship and this brought about the recognition of a need to resolve the long-standing tensions in the company.

It was an unhappy time for everyone. After much heartsearching John decided to cease working in the theatre in order to concentrate on his painting and a more settled married life. In some respects I think he was in any event burnt out as far as Compass was concerned, but for all the people involved the raking of the ashes was not going to be easy, for, although John could not create theatre without us, it was to become clear that Compass could not create theatre without him.

When I left the company that summer I was deeply upset by the break-up of the emotional ties. I gave my last performance with The Compass Players at Stamford Hall, the Co-op College in Leicestershire, and, filled with agonising misery I pirouetted through the part of the pert maidservant Pernille in Holberg's *Times Fool* for the last time. Then I said goodbye to the company.

For a time I wandered about visiting friends. Then one day I was in the National Gallery and who should I meet but our old family friend, the former M.P. Andrew Maclaren, he who had taken an interest in my career three years ago. He helped me to re-establish my confidence, my career and my ambitions.

Later I got a job at the Oldham Coliseum in weekly rep, then I went to Malta with Geoffrey and Laura Kendal and their Shakespeare Theatre Company where, in between learning a part every two days for a month, I even did occasional baby sitting with the young Felicity! Then I made another 'life' decision and, instead of going with them to India, I joined Century Theatre where I worked again with Maurice and Armine. It was there that I met my husband Harold Dellar. He had worked in the Friends' Ambulance Unit after the war and was now recovering from the disillusionment of teacher training. He came down to cook for us, and had two assistant cooks — myself and Henry Livings — as we still followed the principle of doing other work as well as acting.

When we left the Century Theatre we came to Hull where Harold became a lecturer in Social Administration at the University and here we brought up our family. I taught all ages from nursery playgroup to higher education, co-directed Hull Art College Theatre Group with Mike Bradwell (founder of Hull Truck), and acted for B.B.C. North Region. Gradually I became involved in theatre as an expression of community. I set up a Theatre for Children (1963) and after initiating, devising and directing Hull's first Community Play (1974), formed a Community Theatre Workshop with local teachers and amateurs. With Alan Plater, Janet Blackman and others I helped to found the theatre in which Hull Truck is now based and then went on to develop a community arts centre. I have worked throughout as a drama animateur and all the time have drawn upon the skills and understanding that I first acquired during those three years of heightened existence with The Compass Players.

2

ONE FOR THE ROAD

Maurice Daniels

When he was with the Compass Players Maurice Daniels was our company manager as well as taking major acting roles. He then joined the Century Theatre before going to the Royal Shakespeare Company for 27 years, first as assistant director to Peter Hall then as planning controller and development administrator. Recently he has been freelance directing and teaching in American universities and has directed Shakespeare in Hebrew in Tel Aviv. He was given an honorary degree by the University of Birmingham for Services to Shakespeare. In this chapter he concentrates mainly on the educational work of the company and his development of our touring network.

'One for the Road' may perhaps sound like the title for the diary of a dipsomaniac. It does also, however, aptly describe the experiences and recollections of any amongst us, The Compass Players, who elected to join the Company, and found ourselves spending several — in my case six-important years of our lives travelling the highways and, literally, the by-ways of Great Britain. To say that we did this as actors is a true enough but somewhat over-simplistic statement: we all discovered, I think, that there was far more to it than that. And in writing about those years I find that I can only approach it in an autobiographical way, quite simply because everything we did, everything that happened to us, affected us as much as human beings as it affected us as theatre people. Our raison d'être was ostensibly to perform plays, but the framework of life which surrounded this activity was extraordinary in that, within it, we found ourselves in touch with the whole diversity of communities which make up the population of this country. We were received into people's homes, our hosts gave us hospitality sometimes for several nights: we stayed in terraced houses in the mining villages of South Wales, we occasionally 'lorded' it in an elegant country house, we had a taste of what it was like to live in a semi-detached on a housing estate. During those years we met, lived and talked with bank managers, teachers, miners, lawyers, doctors, business men. This was very different from the normal life of an actor who goes into the theatre each night, gives his performance and then goes home; all he can say about his audience is that they were good or awful, or that they laughed or were silent. We were fortunate and learnt something about our audience and the community from which they came.

We also learnt to know our country, as the name of the Company implies, and we did indeed travel to all points of the compass; we might not otherwise have known the Mull of Galloway, the Yorkshire Dales, the strange areas of the Clun valley, the delightful and then unspoilt Kirkcudbrightshire coast. It might perhaps have been years before I found myself in Durham Cathedral, Tewkesbury Abbey or any of the other wonderful churches we made time to visit on our travels: Ely, Canterbury, Wells and others. And almost certainly I would never have known of the existence of places with strange-sounding names like Ystradgynlais, Caersws, Amlwch and Pity Me.

The extraordinary thing, for me anyway, is that all this happened as long ago as 40 years. I am now 72, a time of life when perhaps the memory is not as lively as it has been, and yet now, as I write, the recollection of the years between 1946 and 1952 have a still existing reality and vividness, fragmented though it may be: events, people, journeys, places, disappointments, excitements, deep affections, frictions, doubts, all adding up to a fullness of life which I find still to be very much part of who I am. And the fact that all of us, former Compass Players, wish to and can write about those 'fervent years', which is incidentally the title of a book about the American Group Theatre, seems to me that this must be the same for them too.

So how did it all begin for me? I had been out of the country for nine years — in commerce — and returned home with a decision to be made as to what to do with the rest of my life. It has to be said that I was carrying a fairly heavy guilt-conscience at having been spared any war experience, and I first tried for a job with a refugee organisation. This proved unsuccessful. I then made enquiries about doing a social science degree but was finally daunted by the prospect of three years' study. I needed to be *doing* something. Eventually I asked myself the vital question, 'What have you always wanted to do more than anything else?' and the answer was, as it always had been, 'Theatre'.

Co-incidentally then with my looking at prospectuses of drama schools and looking around for any company with a place for an inexperienced actor — my training was minimal — I saw one day a small advertisement in the *New Statesman* stating that a travelling company was looking for an actor. I applied. Why not? I was invited for an audition, which I duly did for Richard Ward in the tiny sitting-room of a flat in Muswell Hill. I remember that I did Hamlet's speech to Horatio, 'Nay, do not think I flatter...' — a hidden message perhaps for my auditioner, a tall gaunt man, forbidding of exterior but kind of voice. We also chatted about this and that, and the outcome was an invitation to go to South Wales to meet the director, John Crockett, and other members of the Company who were on tour there. I don't recall the name of the mining village where they were playing, only that it was a very hot summer day, and that this delightful welcoming group of people at first encounter looked a pretty scruffy lot, or perhaps a kinder description is 'bohemian'. (I was to remember this some years later when, at one of our company meetings, it was mutually decided that, when on tour it was important for us to look at least tidy even if we fell short of an immediately recognisable respectability!) So there they were, The Compass Players. My first impressions: John, about 6'3" and deceptively tough-looking (he had apparently once been mistaken for Tommy Farr, a heavyweight boxer of the time); Anne, his wife, also tall, and beautiful; Paula, diminutive, sturdily built, with the broadest of smiles and long straggly hair; Elizabeth, with a very county accent; Christina, delightfully diffident; and Leslie, the practical man of the group with the heavy responsibility of keeping the vehicles in working order, and electrician. I suppose I must have had an interview with John but my main impression is still of being with them as a group who I imagined would have their say as to whether I would fit in as a new boy. But most important, and what in itself made the journey worthwhile even if I hadn't been invited to join them, was the performance I saw them give that night; it told me all I needed to know about The Compass Players. The play was *The Quest* by Charles Brasch, a New Zealand poet friend of John; it was indeed a verse play in the form of a modern version of *Everyman*. In addition to the spare fine writing there was music, and dance to music culled from Berlioz' *Symphonie Fantastique*. To this day I cannot hear it without having instant recall of the production which I was later to stage-manage. The costumes were simple and colourful — cloaks and tunics. It was exciting to watch and listen to, and it was something I had not expected, that is to meet a company who, without sudsidy of any sort, had the courage and certainty of belief in this kind of theatre to do it rather than the more conventional 'well-made' play to audiences up and down the country for many of whom it was their first experience of theatre. I responded to it in a particularly positive way as it was the kind of theatre I knew and liked best. As an actor with a small amateur Little Theatre group in Manchester, the Unnamed Society, I had been in plays like Cocteau's *Orphée*, the first amateur production of T. S. Eliot's *Murder in the Cathedral, The Tempest* and others of that ilk. This was the kind of theatre I wanted to be part of: simple staging, a richness of text, music, and a company of actors who were committed, and whose enjoyment of what they were doing was shared with the audience.

I was an even happier man when, not long afterwards, I was invited to join the company. Conditions of employment were simple; to act, and to do as everybody else did, which meant taking on any other responsibilities for which I might be fitted and, as it turned out, if I wasn't fitted for them I'd have to learn about them, as I did with the inside of an internal combustion engine when I became Transport Manager. The financial arrangements were even simpler: 15 shillings a week (in modern parlance 75p!) plus that well-worn phrase 'All found'; in practical terms this meant one was guaranteed food and a bed to sleep in at all times, which for an actor even nowadays are conditions not to be sneezed at. All members of the company received that same financial reward of 15 shillings per week which was, of course, then worth more than 75p today, and looking for some magic formula for conversioin into present-day values, I can only come up with the comparative values, then and now, of a two-ounce bar of Cadbury's milk chocolate. On this basis I reckon we received the equivalent of £9 per week. Were we foolhardy? Were we dedicated? Neither of these, I think, came into consideration.

And so I made my first acquaintance with the wonderful headquarters of The Compass Players, The Warren, a large rambling house deep in the heart of Gloucestershire and a (long) walkable distance from Tintern Abbey. It stood on a hill at the end of a half-mile long drive, with an age-old wistaria by the front door whose roots spread underneath the entrance hall pushing up the tiles; a front terrace with a view for many miles and a continuation of the hill, densely wooded, rising sharply at the back. Flower beds and a large vegetable garden which we looked after, down two flights of stone steps and near our neighbours, a farming community led by George Ineson, also a friend of John. There we lived, coldly in winter (crouched over a paraffin stove in one's room learning lines), though warm in the main room which had a large welcoming fireplace where we burnt mostly wood which we had sawn ourselves. In summer it was an ideal place to live. And there we also worked... and worked... and worked; rehearsing in what was probably the original drawing-room, making what little scenery we needed, props, costumes and sometimes even wigs. These were ideal working conditions for a theatre company: our own rehearsal spaces and working facilities, being able to work whenever we wanted to (no Equity restrictions), in constant and immediate consultation about how the productions were developing, no distractions from the outside world, and plenty of fresh air on tap. It was perhaps for these reasons that Jacques Copeau, the famous French director, decided in the mid-twenties to leave his well-established theatre and reputation in Paris and move his company to a large house in the country.

Working in schools

But every two or three months we had to leave our house in the country, and it was with a mixture of relief, eagerness and reluctance that we exchanged the intensity of the final weeks of rehearsals for the pressure of a pretty formidable schedule: what might be described as a mini nationwide tour with an average of six performances a week, and in a different place almost every day. Days on which we had only an evening performance presented no problems of any great importance, and we were generally able to arrive with sufficient time to cope with any that might arise. But on recollection, our work in schools was the most demanding in terms of planning, travelling and unexpected problems — like school lunches in the hall where we were to play, though we soon got used to that; above all it was the pressure of time as we were faced with matinees starting at 1.30 p.m. so that children could catch their school buses at the end of the show. But the pressure had started several hours earlier. A typical day began with the rendezvous at 9 a.m. to leave us time to arrive at the school immediately after morning assembly, having found the right entrance and parked the van. That was the plan which could, however, be fraught with various kinds of snags: it could happen that we were all staying in different parts of the town as guests of hospitable members of staff and their friends which might indeed mean that some us of would already be at the school at 9 a.m. waiting for the others. But the others had to find their way in a strange town and, with the best of intentions, not everybody had managed to clock in on time, added to which we all learned to live with the fact of life that some are born punctual, some achieve punctuality, and some have punctuality thrust upon them. The final hazard of all, however, to our well-intentioned planning was finding *that* school which occasionally took us as long to reach as we had taken for a ten or fifteen-mile journey the previous evening. Firstly, schools are rarely on a main road, and secondly, after having enlisted the help of a passer-by, we found ourselves at a school with the right name but for the wrong age-group or sex. And so the minutes ticked by, but by and large, to all our credit, we were left with only the normal pressure of getting the show ready in an unknown venue in three hours.

This started with the unloading of the van — in boys' schools hopefully with the help of some willing and strapping sixth-formers — and the manhandling of hampers, screens and lights to wherever they had to be. The distance from where the van was parked varied enormously. Once everything was in place, each one of us to our allotted tasks; the women ironing and doing running repairs on the costumes, two men on lights and the rest setting up the stage. When John was not on tour with us I was front man or head boy — being a decade older than most of the others — and I had to play a co-ordinating role before joining the stage crew. This involved liaising with various members of staff about detailed organisation, where we had to go for lunch, where the dressing rooms were *etc.*, *etc.* And, of course, there was the meeting with the Caretaker — capital letter for the figure of power in the school, particularly when it came to discussing what was to be done with the piano sitting stage centre. More than once I have been met with the pronouncement that 'that piano has to stay where it is'. But when that piano was a grand piano and competed so intrusively on a not very large stage with the modest area we needed for our hessian-covered screens something had to be done. Diplomacy didn't always work, and occasionally a little brinkmanship was required, like the truthful sanction that the show could not happen if the offending piano stayed on stage and, sometimes through recourse to a member of staff, permission was given for the piano to be removed...by us, with the proviso that we also put it back. You had to be fit to be a Compass Player.

We visited several hundred schools — Senior High, Grammar and Public — during my six years with the Company and, unfailingly, one of the most interesting aspects of the day was the morning's preparation for the performance, for it was then that we developed an insight into the general character of the school to the point where we often had a not totally inaccurate idea of what kind of audience it would yield. Perhaps because we were theatre people we found ourselves peculiarly sensitive to the prevailing human ambience which became discernible in many passing details: apart from the degree of co-operation we received we were aware of the way people looked at us and spoke to us — were we there as intruders or as guests? It was, for instance, an encouraging sign if we found doors being held open for us by children as we walked along crowded corridors during a break. A small thing, perhaps, but a spontaneous gesture like that told us, in a very simple way, something positive about that community: rather than a mere act of politeness it represented the natural social grace of being aware of other human beings, and it appeared to be a normal thing for them to do. This could only have come from an enlightened leadership that considered education as something that goes beyond classroom work. It was also confirmed on the many occasions when the Head, in his role as host, took time off to meet and chat with us over mid-morning coffee, or in the friendly atmosphere of the staff common room where people showed a genuine interest in what we were doing, our choice of play, and indeed in us as human beings. By and large, this was the kind of reception we were given, and it boded well for the afternoon's performance, but there were variations in the treatment. At the other end of the spectrum I remember one occasion when, as we were shown into the staffroom we were greeted with nothing more cordial than a flicked formal smile, or a nod as somebody looked up from the newspaper he was reading; and for us that was a danger signal about the audience we were to meet. There was, too, a girls' school where, as soon as a member of staff appeared in the corridor, the girls stood silently against the wall with eyes modestly cast downwards until the teacher had passed. We did not expect an uninhibited response from that audience, rightly in the event. But those experiences only stay in the mind because they were exceptions, and my over-riding recollections of our school work are those of hospitality and many unsolicited gestures of care and concern for our well-being. High among these is the memorable remark of a not-so-young woman teacher to two of our girls as they were lugging a particularly

55

heavy costume hamper along a particularly long corridor. She stopped them. 'Ladies,' she said, 'you shouldn't be doing this — do remember, you are future mothers of England. I will get someone to help you.' She did, and thus achieved private immortality amongst all Compass Players. 'Future mothers of England' is a phrase we will never forget. It also made me wryly aware that no such concern was shown towards the male members of the Company; nobody pointed out to us as we struggled with a diabolically heavy and ill-balanced switch-board (my unfavourite piece of equipment) that we were future fathers of England! However, this is what several of us have managed to become, and we have survived to tell the tale.

And then, of course, there was the School Lunch. Food-wise as they say, we put schools into two categories: those where we had the usual education department institution lunch — meat (kind of), two maltreated veg, followed by stodge pudding and custard; and those where we were given Special Treatment. The latter meant that either our friendly host teacher or the Head had a natural sense of hospitality *and* knew how important food is to actors and had enlisted the help of the domestic science teacher. She, in turn, had commandeered that morning's cooking class to prepare a junior *cordon bleu* luncheon. Now, for those of us with particularly energetic or demanding parts in the show due to begin very soon afterwards, this was something of a tease; it has to be said that the food generally won, but even if it didn't and one was strong enough to resist that pristine-looking lemon meringue pie, it was the thought that counted. And good thoughts were much appreciated.

So finally to the reason for our being there: the performance. What were they actually going to be like? In spite of any expectations or warnings we might have had, we knew that school audiences could be wonderful or they could be hell, and anyway it was always a risk. Much of the responsibility for minimising that risk was ours, but even with that in mind we had run the whole gamut from having toffee papers and the like thrown at us to seeing a group of eager, excited children wanting to talk to us at the end of the performance, and even asking for our autographs — no better way of bolstering an actor's ego. Generally the group personality of our audience matched up with what we had gleaned from the three or four hours we had spent amongst them. Our pragmatism had stood us in good stead.

It also led us to have our favourite schools — for reasons other than the excellence of their catering. We even had a favourite area of the country as far as schools were concerned: this was the North East, and in particular County Durham where a friendly and enlightened County Drama Organiser, Dorothy Carr, believed in our work to the extent of booking us, several years in succession, for a series of performances in schools in her area. Amongst these was one I think we probably all remember, Bishop Auckland Grammar School where we regularly had one of the best audiences we found anywhere. Our day there was always rounded-off with a get-together with the sixth formers, boys and girls, when over cups of tea — and probably home-made angel cakes — we had a discussion about the play and the production, and they asked us questions about it. There was one occasion when the tables were turned and we had to ask them a question. We had just played Marlowe's *Dr Faustus* and, as always, they had been an exemplary audience: lively but always listening, and creating a quality of silence which actors thrive on and to which they are gratefully sensitive. In this production, however, that silence was broken for a few moments at a point in the play which has a kind of magic about it with the famous speech, 'Was this the face that launched a thousand ships?' — the appearance of Helen of Troy. In this production Faustus approached her and kissed her on the lips, quite chastely. When that happened the atmosphere in the audience was immediately disturbed; there was a shuffling of chairs, there might even have been the odd giggle. So we taxed them with it and asked them why they thought this had happened in an afternoon when, apart from this, we felt we had their complete and rapt attention. An embarrassed silence followed and then came a quiet, subdued and succinct answer from a shy-looking youth, 'Well, I suppose you could put it down to sex and adolescence.' So we then talked about it freely and it emerged that for those few moments — a man and a woman kissing — it was related to what they see in films and on film posters, and even this intimation of sexuality — chaste as it was — was something they found difficult to share as a mixed group of teenagers. We thought no less of them for that and they remained one of our most looked-forward-to dates, as did the North East as a whole.

This leads me to a digression from 'A Day in the Life of a Compass Player' fragmented as it is — which, however, is not totally irrelevant as it relates those experiences in the North East forty years ago to a much more recent period — the mid-1970's. During the time I worked with the Royal Shakespeare Company one of my responsibilities was to organise the yearly visit to Newcastle-upon-Tyne, where the company has played a six weeks' season since 1977. Apart from the main productions in the Theatre Royal and at the University Gulbenkian studio theatre there are many extra-mural activities, among which figured an extensive education programme consisting of visits to schools and colleges for question and answer sessions, workshops and open rehearsals. What I found fascinating was that, from the very first year — and I went there six times — each Stratford company was bowled over by the quality of the reception of everything they did: the lively non-reverential response to Shakespeare, the interest, intelligence and enthusiasm of schoolchildren and their teachers in discussions and the overall feeling of being appreciated for their own worth. It was, for me, a confirmation of my own impression of that area: that the North East has an energy and ethos of its own. I like to think that, among all the people up there who saw the R.S.C. productions, there could have been a fair smattering of adults who, as children, had their first taste of theatre from The Compass Players. A goodly thought. This was brought home to me even more one evening when I was leaving the Theatre Royal stage door. There was a group of students armed with autograph books waiting for the actors to emerge. One of them, somewhat older than the rest, eagerly held out her book to me. 'I don't think you want mine,' I said. 'I'm not an actor.' 'I know,' she replied. 'You're Maurice Daniels and you came to our school.' I signed her book.

So back to The Compass Players and their school work, an important part of the year's programme on which we depended considerably — as do many companies — for our income. John Crockett's concern to combine elements of education with the entertainment value of the show was always present, and with it the awareness that words alone are not enough to keep young audiences interested and involved, so there was always music and dance in the school programmes. When I joined the company the school show in the repertoire consisted of an episode from a mediaeval Mystery play, a thread of the story in *Twelfth Night* which was called *Malvolio Mock'd*, and a charming Commedia dell'Arte mime performed by John, Anne and Paula — all accomplished dancers — to music by Marcello; there was a fourth piece whose title escapes me. These 'Gems from World Drama', so to speak, were interspersed with introductions spoken by one of the actors in a long cloak who came in front of the curtain to explain where the next piece came from, who the author was, period in history *etc.* (This also allowed time for minimal scene and costume changes to take place.) This format worked in a well-intentioned kind of way, but the children were quick to suss out that these commentaries smacked more of teaching than theatre; the disguise was not skillful enough — something was lacking in terms of theatrical continuity and therefore of entertainment value. John then devised a programme with a similar pattern, i.e. it contained several different pieces which were presented in their chronological order, but this time with a theme for the whole show which was the story of the Fool in the theatre through the ages. It was called *The Jester*. Although again there were commentaries on each piece, a continuity was kept by having these spoken autobiographically by the actor playing The Fool who appeared, in different guises, in most of the pieces. This show, with many songs and dances appealed to a wide age-range of school audiences and, exhausting though it was with only five of us, the audience response made it highly enjoyable to play.

The next development was to find complete plays to offer to schools, and again we had John to thank for the first step in that direction. He wrote, for our company of seven, a highly-coloured and remarkably dramatic adaptation of Chaucer's *The Pardoner's Tale*, again with dance and music — this time Stravinsky's *The Rite of Spring*. We were uncompromising if nothing else. The cautionary message from the Pardoner himself, '*Radix malorum est cupiditas*', or, in the words of the popular song, 'Money is the root of all evil', seemed an appropriate one for children (and indeed for adults). We then took the plunge further into the classics with Milton's *Comus* and Marlowe's *Dr Faustus* for which we increased the size of the company to nine people. *Comus* had music by Lawes and his contemporaries, and Richard Strauss' *Ein Heldenleben* provided a brilliant musical framework for *Dr Faustus*.

These latter two shows again included mime and dance as an important part of the action and it is an appropriate moment to say a word or two about Anne Crockett's contribution to the company's work. Not only did she have an unerring flair for finding the right composer and piece, and culling from it what was needed for particular moments, mimes and dances; she was also our long-suffering and inspiring choreographer. I think it is true to say that when each of us joined the company our dancing skills (and that word is an exaggeration in itself) varied from the inept to the mediocre, and that way they would have remained had it not been for Anne. She limbered us up — daily and painfully — taught us and somehow managed to mould us into a group that could move in time to music, that became aware of what unexpected movements arms, legs and bodies were capable of and, if nothing else, was committed to trying to do justice to her always highly inventive choreography. I still like to remember that I was taught stage dancing by somebody who had been trained by somebody who had danced with Martha Graham's company. A modest pedigree.

But to return to the subject of our repertoire in general. Looking at the list of plays we took out on the road to our unsuspecting and often theatrically naïve audiences, I am amazed and inordinately proud of our temerity of choice. I say 'our' choice, but I know that without John's guidance and vision, his focus on our *raison d'être* and his justified bullying, the list would have been far less distinguished. He helped us to be aware of the unique advantages we had as a theatre company: (a) we were visiting our audiences, on average, only once a year and therefore if they liked us they were prepared to take what we had to offer, (b) we were not dependent on box-office receipts as we received a guaranteed minimum fee (with sometimes, all too rarely, a small share of the take over and above that fee), (c) the plays could stay in the repertoire as long as there were new places to be visited where they had not been seen and (d) with out simple style of staging we could go out on the road with five or six different productions packed into that long-suffering vehicle so aptly named Bertha. But perhaps more relevant than anything else was our own artistic well-being for which we needed to be doing plays in which we believed and which, therefore, we could perform with a degree of passion, thereby enjoying a sense of fulfilment.

One shrinks at the cliché 'plays with a message', but I think it is true to say that the serious plays we did were not irrelevant to the human condition, their values were universal and, mostly, they had a richness of language that was worth speaking and listening to. It could perhaps be said that we were arrogant in declining to give audiences 'what they wanted', but I think this is only the negative side of believing that they would want what we had to offer when they had experienced it. This was obviously not always the case, but even so there were only two possible consequences: either they did enjoy what they saw and said please come back again, or they did not like it, in which case we did not go back there and we peddled our wares in hitherto unexplored areas.

Planning the tours

I realise at this moment that I have made no mention about how we found ourselves at all points of the compass in England, Scotland and Wales. Planning and booking the tours was a lengthy and complex process and became one of those 'other responsibilities' I was deputed to take on, partly perhaps because there was no one else to do it, and partly putting to good use the administrative organisational experience I had had during my years in commerce. As Tours Manager, in consultation with John and Anne who had been on the road for two years when I joined the company, we decided — at least on paper — which areas we would make for during that particular two or three months' nationwide tour. And this would be a tour of mainly one-night stands with an occasional luxury of a whole week at the Library Theatre, Manchester. We needed an average of six performances a week (including school matinées) to come as near as we could to breaking even financially. 'Overdraft' was a word that was not unknown to us. Financially there were no funds (nor time) for travelling expenses to allow me to travel round the country 'selling' The Compass Players except for one period when we were in such dire financial straits that it was decided I should withdraw from the acting strength and go out and book a tour in west Wales — a new area. It was a delightful experience, and travelling by bus I discovered the beauties of the Mawddach estuary near Dolgelly and saw, for the very first time, the wonderful Cader Idris range of mountains. However, with that exception, we had to convince people — individual schools, Education Authorities, local Arts societies and others — mostly by *correspondence* and with our advance publicity, that we were worth paying 15 guineas a show for, that we were not a wild bunch of dropouts, that we were serious in our intentions and our performances, and that we were offering classy stuff. One of the many things which had impressed me when I joined the company was the quality of its advance publicity leaflet: the printing, Times Roman type-face (which we stuck to) in blue on high quality paper, as simple as that, but of great importance as it created the right impression immediately and, hopefully, gave the receiver some idea of what the company was about. Later we graduated to a small illustrated brochure with two-colour printing and photographs of several productions. All this was expensive but as an investment was invaluable. As for the actual booking of dates, finding a continuous itinerary, allowing time to change areas, ensuring a minimum weekly number of performances, this meant letters, letters and more letters, mostly handwritten as our typewriter hardly merited its name. Some of these fell on stony ground, some remained unanswered, but over the years there was enough response to develop a touring network which yielded many return bookings and provided us with work for six years. It was perhaps made a little easier coming immediately after the war during which travelling companies had been gratefully accepted in many parts of the country. Indeed, some of the leading actors of the British theatre were to be seen in regions where there had possibly been no professional theatre of quality: Dame Sybil Thorndike playing Medea in the Welsh mining towns, Robert Donat and others. These were government-sponsored tours under the auspices of C.E.M.A. — Council for the Encouragement of Music and the Arts — later to burgeon into the Arts Council of Great Britain. Against this, however, there were a few companies who were not helpful ambassadors of travelling theatre, whose work was shoddy and who appeared not to care about the quality of their shows, thus implying a lack of concern for their audiences. They made it difficult sometimes for us to assure people — sight unseen — that we were of an acceptable degree of normality, and for them to understand that, 'different' though actors may be, they are actually human beings. This may sound far-fetched but perhaps the following account may serve to illustrate the point. We were in a village hall where the company was hard at work setting up the stage, lights etc., and I was in the small entrance hall on a step ladder hanging up publicity photographs before joining the others. A lady came in and, hearing the hammering and sounds of men at work, asked the caretaker what was happening, and he informed her that there was a 'group of strolling players' who were going to do a play that night. She then caught sight of me and enquired in a gently rolling Welsh lilt, 'Is that one of them?' 'Yes,' he replied. And then, in one of the loudest stage whispers I have heard, she said, 'Oh! I've never been so near one before.' I was almost tempted to look down to see whether my forked tail was protruding from my trouser bottoms. There is also the story — truly not apocryphal — of a landlady in a town visited regularly by a regional theatre company who always had the same actor stay with her as a lodger, and who was known to have confided to a friend, 'You know, when Jack stays here I always lock my bedroom door.' So even as recently as forty years ago, the label 'Rogues and Vagabonds' was still extant.

But gradually over the years, as the work of the Compass Players became known, indifference and prejudice made way for increasing support and encouragement. Without these we might not have had the sturdiness of spirit to continue and accept what, in any other context, could be described sometimes as a pretty gruelling existence. And it could be pretty tough going, rootless and permanently peripatetic. At its worst it did verge on the intolerable, like on a freezing cold morning, with a schools matinée to do, the five men in the company lining up to take turns with the starting handle to crank up our recalcitrant Bertha. At times like that it was not unreasonable to wonder why we were doing it. Some journeys were pretty boring too, and I remember one occasion when my enthusiasm took a sudden nose dive. It was a pelting wet Stygian Sunday evening as we travelled from Gloucestershire to Middlesborough, some 250 miles. There were no motorways in those days so we had to travel through the suburbs of several large towns. I looked at the drawn curtains of people's sitting rooms and imagined how infinitely preferable it would be sitting in front of a fire, safe and warm (we had no heater in our van) with the Sunday papers and television. And of course it would have been, but then the thought of our destination and what awaited us there quickly dispelled these nagging doubts about our way of life. We were on our way to Ormesby Hall, the beautiful 18th-century country house, now a National Trust property but then the home of Colonel and Mrs Pennyman. He was a retired regular army soldier, silver-haired with matching toothbrush moustache and a tanned bald pate. He was invariably in tweeds, and underneath that head-thrust-forward, apparently peppery exterior, beat the kindest of hearts. He was the quintessential hunting, fishing Tory squire. His wife Ruth, a witty, highly-intelligent and gracious lady — and a Socialist to boot — was the leader of their partnership as voluntary patrons of the arts and we were grateful for their warm patronage. There had been others before us including, incongruously enough, the Theatre Workshop Company with strong Communist Party connections under the leadership of the indomitable and now almost legendary Joan Littlewood. They were allowed to use, as their headquarters, the converted stable block. We were more fortunate, not I must quickly add because of any political affiliations either way, but, because we were infrequent visitors, we were received as paying guests in the Pennyman's home. It was there that we tasted the delights of gracious living: four-poster beds, all in single rooms and a luxury to be cherished, breakfast in the spacious tall-windowed dining room overlooking a formal rose garden, hot plates on the sideboard with freshly cooked (even for late-comers) bacon and eggs and sometimes even kedgeree. And when we came back from an evening performance there would be hot soup on the Aga, and bread and cheese and cocoa and...hot water bottles in our beds.

This kind of concern for our well-being was rich compensation for the more rigorous times in our journeying. We felt cared for: we were made to feel special. And taken all in all, we were special — not perhaps unique — but special. Some of our hosts used to say to us, 'You're just like J.B.Priestley's *The Good Companions*,' at which we would cringe. Our reaction was really a bit snobbish, if not arrogant, and was simply because we did not like being compared with anybody else. We were who we were.

But, yes, we were good companions, warts and all: seven (at one time nine) individuals, working, living and travelling as a community, sharing experiences that affected any one or all of us, sharing a common belief in what we were doing and how we were doing it. It had become a way of life.

If this is the case — a way of life — why then did it not continue beyond those six years? In looking for an answer to this question and reading what I have written so far, I realise that this account of The Compass Players may have sounded more like a hagiography than a biography.. But haloes were not part of our personal equipment. None of us deluded ourselves, I am sure, into thinking that, strong as the bond was between us as a community, this rendered us immune from normal human frailties, nor did it absolve us from normal human responsibilities. So. Accepting that communal living in any form presents its own particular problems, is it possible that in a community of actors these problems can be exacerbated? The actor's ego, an essential part of his artistic psyche, is sensitized in a special kind of way by the demands made on it; and the extremes of emotion — albeit expressed mostly in fantasy form, the theatre — have to be more readily accessible than for most people. Fantasy and reality living at close quarters. I think we were intuitively aware of all this and therefore our individual foibles and inadequacies, passions and vulnerabilities were mutually absorbed in a kind of symbiosis, while still recognising the need for each to be his own person, for the well-being of the group. But what I think we were not conscious of was the paradox of this ambience which could allow, even create, an emotional climate for relationships to develop more deeply than a more 'normal' pattern of living. I was one of the protagonists in those emotional cross-currents and therefore instrumental in revealing the crisis of a 'new' reality that could not be ignored or glossed over for the sake of the company's work. A logical solution, and one that had been used before, would have been to replace anybody who left; but the problem was not a simple one. It had reached the point of disturbing and finally disrupting the balance of this particular group of human beings of like mind. It led, in fact, to the break-up of The Compass Players.

Writing about this some forty years later — and with no intention of defensiveness or expiation of responsibilities — has clarified for me what was probably the true nature of The Compass Players, and why it became necessary for us to disband.

We had been something other than just a group of actors with a common artistic ideal. We were not unique in that; many companies aim for and achieve that. Where we differed, I now think, was that our work was so ineluctably related to our group existence that when *that* was lost its corporate heartbeat (clumsy, pompous sounding words but I can find no others) our artistic ethos was robbed of its immediate meaning. Who we were became more important than what we did. So we disbanded in the spring of 1952, sadly, but knowing that there was no alternative to redress the deep imbalance of the situation. We all went our separate ways. Several of us have stayed in touch and meet, not regularly or in any kind of formal reunion, but enough to know that the strangeness of the passing of time has not made strangers of us. More importantly, neither has it negated the spirit of The Compass Players.

It needs to be recorded too that this spirit would not have been born, would not have prospered without the vision and tenacity of a remarkable human being, John Crockett, an extraordinary maverick from a traditional English upper-class background endowed with more creative talents than it is fair for one person to possess: painter, writer, actor, director, designer and mask-maker *par excellence*. His artistic values were uncompromising, their integrity unimpeachable and these were reflected in all his theatre work. As a director he was both demanding and encouraging but with an acutely suspicious eye and ear for the spurious in acting: the short cut, the effect rather than the cause. We learned from him a respect for the text, classical or modern, and perhaps more important than anything else, how to listen on stage. His criteria for the finished product — the play — even with our limited technical resources were of the highest, and even with our undeveloped talents as actors his productions had a clarity of intention, a cleanness of line and drew from us vitality which sprang naturally from the enjoyment of what we were doing and our belief in it. John was a dynamo of creative energy and human contradictions: patient and of an infuriating intolerance, high ebullient good humour and a lower flash-point than most people have, but his occasional moods of gloomy depression were out-balanced by an excoriating sense of humour and a zest for life that was delightfully infectious. He was never dull to be with. My favourite mind-picture of John is of him sitting at his easel in the large sunny rehearsal room at The Warren, listening to a cricket match commentary on the radio while he was finishing the detailed, almost tedious brush-work on one of his deeply religious paintings. Len Hutton scoring a century and the Resurrection as simultaneous happenings!

So to end, as I began, on an autobiographical note. I left the company a richer person (in everything but money!) than I had six years before. My experiences had provided me with enough temerity and confidence to apply for a job as stage-manager with the Royal Shakespeare Company, though ready to accept that with virtually no knowledge of the inner workings of a large theatre organisation I would probably not be eligible. I was wrong. It would appear that my years of coping with unpredictable problems of one-night stands, of dealing with caretakers and grand pianos, of meeting so many different kinds of people, the theatre skills and values I had acquired — all these stood me in good stead and I was marketable. Two months after my interview I found myself as stage-manager for productions of *King Lear* and *Much Ado About Nothing* with Sir John Gielgud and Dame Peggy Ashcroft, and it was for a tour: Austria, Switzerland, Germany, Denmark,

Norway, Newcastle, Edinburgh *etc., etc.* I was on the road again. I worked with the company for 27 years during which time I had the good fortune to learn about and eventually be responsible for several of the company's artistic and administrative activities. In my final years these included setting up an education programme. I was back in schools again. In 1982 I retired from the R.S.C. and since then have been travelling in America teaching and directing Shakespeare, mostly in university theatre departments.

I mention these details less as a chronicle of personal events than as an extension of those first years in the professional theatre, and now, working with student actors who also help to make the set, paint the scenery, sew costumes, rig lights, I feel I have come full circle. And I am still 'on the road' or — and perhaps in more than one sense — in the air.

Finally, two codas, both of which are reflections of life with The Compass Players. Coda one: while I was in New York last December I went to the wonderful Big Apple Circus. As I reached my seat I was greeted by one of their clowns, gentle-faced and of manner. He welcomed me and as we chatted I discerned a slight foreign accent, so as he was leaving me I said, 'May I ask where you come from?' His reply, with the ghost of a smile: 'Well, I come from the past, and after the show I shall be travelling into the future.'

The words of the second coda are from Jean-Louis Barrault: The peculiar charm of the theatre is...

to live with the rogues because one is in love with Justice,

to sink with the rogues so as to preserve Health,

to tremble with those in dread in order to find a little Happiness,

to be always braving death because one loves only Life,

to move off without rest, suitcase in hand, rucksack on back, in order to try to understand

and from fear of one day arriving.

another asked me to show my legs. They were scornful of the glossy photos (cut-price for students!) I took with me. I wrote to dozens of repertory companies to no avail (although most of them replied, if I sent an S.A.E.).

Pam went off to help a small touring theatre company at their headquarters in Gloucestershire during their summer rehearsal period. The house was called The Warren. She wrote to say that she was having a wonderful time doing all sorts of odd jobs and had also been helping make hay for a nearby farm. When I had a letter a few weeks later to say she was joining this company, The Compass Players. I thought she was a little mad!

I managed to get a small job in an excellent production of *The Cherry Orchard* at the Arts Theatre. Jean Anderson was Madame Ranevsky. Sybil Ewbank, whose mother, Eileen Thorndyke, had taught us at Central, was also in it (she was later to join The Compass Players). We ran on and off as maidservants in the first and last acts, carrying baggage, and were guests at the party in between. After this, seeing no other hope of work, I answered an advertisement in *The Stage* for a job as juvenile lead in Brighton for £8 a week. An agent asked me to call but the job turned out to be in Blackburn at a twice nightly weekly rep. The contract was 'suspect' but in desperation I decided to sign it. I was now a probationary member of Equity and there was only a short time until the end of the season. With all my belongings in a trunk I set off for Blackburn, having written to the stage manager to ask him to fix 'digs'.

I arrived at the Grand Theatre in time for the first performance of *Jane Eyre* on the Monday night. It was quite dreadful. (I found out later that this first house each Monday served as the dress rehearsal.) When the orchestra suddenly launched into melodramatic music at the entrance of Rochester's mad wife I wanted to go back to London! The stage manager, a girl called Astrid, told me the 'digs' were so awful she had arranged for me to share a room at the Y.W.C.A with her. We were later joined by another actress called Sarn A'deane.

The next few weeks were incredible. We presented a different play every week with performances at 5 p.m. and 8 p.m. each night. We never had a proper 'read through' and only rehearsed in the mornings. I learnt my lines more or less accurately, but found the 'cue' scripts we often used extremely unnerving. It was a nightmare only to have one line (or less) of the speech before my own (the cue) printed on the page. There was no indication of how many other people had spoken since my character last said anything or what had been going on. It was all the more difficult as some of the others only gave the gist of what they should be saying which often didn't match what was on the paper. This certainly taught one to listen carefully and to be inventive! Our mid-morning refreshment consisted of strong tea, heavily sweetened with saccharine, which an ASM brought from a café next door in a chipped enamel jug. We drank it out of 'prop' cups (usually cracked) and even jam jars. The theatre itself was old and dirty and had a horrid smell.

The company was one of a number run by Frank Fortescue, and several of the actors had worked for him for years. He was very good to his 'regulars' and they adored him and spoke of him in hushed voices. I was introduced to him once, in the wings during a performance, and can only remember a rather limp handshake. There were two married couples in the company who played the older 'character' parts and had trunks filled with useful props, wigs and bits of costume. They knew all the traditional 'business' for plays like *East Lynne* and were very helpful to me when I found myself playing Lady Isobel (a huge part) for two performances only during the last week of the season! They were real 'pros' in the same way that The Crummles were in *Nicholas Nickleby* and on several occasions gave extremely moving performances. The 'producer' also acted, but, whenever he could, disappeared to the front of the house (in full make-up) and when he next appeared on stage smelt strongly of beer. One of the married men, well past his prime, sometimes played the romantic lead and, having never rehearsed the love scenes, would, in performance, clasp the poor girl playing juvenile lead in a vice-like grip and smother her with kisses. She was at his mercy in front of the audience! Our audience was, in fact, very loyal and by the end of the week we had full houses.

Just before the end of the season, Pam wrote to say that The Compass Players were going to play at a school in Blackburn and that one of the actresses was leaving. Why didn't I write to John Crockett? I did. He came to see me in a piece called *The Rotters* and asked me to meet him next day for tea at his cousin's house where we talked and he told me how the company was organised. Everyone got 15/- a week and their 'keep' and all necessary expenses were paid from a general fund. There would be company meetings from time to time at which everyone could express his or her opinion and each actor had to help with stage management and other tasks. He asked me if I would like to act with the company and take on the job of wardrobe mistress but suggested I went to see *The Pardoner's Tale* the next afternoon before finally making up my mind.

At lunchtime the following day I arrived back at the Y.W.C.A. canteen to find Sarn in a state of great excitement. 'THEY'VE been here!' 'Who?' 'The Compass Players — having lunch.' 'How do you know?' 'Oh, you could TELL. They came in a big blue van and there was this ACTOR — he had a most SATURNIC (sic) expression. Oooh! There they ARE!' I looked up and there, waiting at the traffic lights was the van. A lean, dark-haired man was driving. He wore a long yellow scarf.

Later that afternoon I sat at the back of the school hall. The audience was buzzing with excitement and there was a smell I was soon to know almost too well — a smell of chalk and ink and gym-shoes and sweat. From the moment I heard the opening bars of Stravinsky's music, I was sitting on the edge of my seat and so was the rest of the audience. I was bowled over by the use of colour in the costumes and the lighting — mostly gold and amber —

the simple sets of plain hessian screens which contrasted with the deep blue of the cyclorama; the cut-out tree; the masks; the quality of the acting and especially the dances. Yes, I did want to join the company!

When the play was over, I was introduced to Maurice Daniels (whom I recognised as the driver), Hedley Lunn and Moira Deady. I already knew Martin Heller and Dorothy Grumbar (the actress who was leaving) from Central School days. I helped load the van and then joined everyone for company high tea, prepared by Pam, before going back to the theatre. I no longer cared about the awful *Rotters* and the one-day marathon of *East Lynn* — I was going to be a Compass Player.

After the final performance at Blackburn I went round saying goodbye to everyone. *East Lynne* had been a great success and many of the audience were in tears in spite of Little Willie being played by a rather plump local girl dressed in boys striped pyjamas! One of the stage-hands (I didn't know his name) called down from the flies, 'Goodbye, Miss, and I 'ope you live to be a bloody 'undred!' One of the most heartwarming compliments I ever received. Perhaps my weeks in Blackburn had not been wasted after all!

A few days before Christmas I set out for Gloucestershire. While I was waiting for the train to Lydney on Gloucester station a young man joined me and asked if I was going to The Warren as he was too. We travelled together along the banks of the Severn Estuary. It was already dark and a beautiful night. Suddenly he asked if we could have the light off so that we could see the moonlight on the river. Having been told never to speak to strange men I was extremely uneasy but convinced myself that it must be all right as he knew The Warren! And so, in darkness, we arrived at Lydney. The adventure had begun!

A taxi had been sent to meet us and carried us through the winding lanes and along the bumpy drive to the car park below the house. I climbed up the steps and tapped nervously at the door. A woman carrying a baby opened it. She gave me a lovely, warm welcome and introduced herself as Anne, John's wife, and the baby as Lizzy. Brushing aside my rather half-hearted offer, she paid the taxi, explaining that this was a necessary expense and the only way to get from the station. The Company wasn't back yet or the van would have come.

In the living room the wooden table was set for supper and a cheerful log fire was burning at the far end of the room. I noticed a recessed niche in the wall — a holy-water stoup or perhaps a place for tinder or a candle? But what really struck me were the pictures on the walls, the first Crocketts I had seen. I was particularly impressed by the one hanging over the fireplace. It was of a sinewy, bronzed young man lying on a vibrant deep-blue cloak with a young woman. The grass beneath them was specked with little flowers and she was heavily pregnant. John had painted the baby in her womb in soft, pearly colours with delicate, swirling brush strokes. I had never seen anything quite like it before. Anne said, jokingly, that her mother had said

70

it should have a little curtain to draw across the centre, but I was excited by it. It is named *Creation*.

Soon after that the Compass Players arrived, bursting in with all their assorted bags and suitcases, glad to be back after the long, cold journey and hungry and tired. Anne had prepared a hot meal and all through supper she was regaled with stories and anecdotes about what had happened — good, bad and amusing — on the tour. This scene was repeated many times during my days with the company (I can't remember what happened to the young man!).

Pam and I again shared a room. It was simply furnished and the beds were very basic but I soon got used to my pale-green cotton sleeping bag (ex-youth hostel), and in the morning I was able to see for the first time the view from the gothic windows, right down over the woods to the Severn Estuary. I never grew tired of that view. It varied each day with the changing light and the seasons. In the summer, the room was filled with the sweet dusty smell of the wistaria which grew all along the front of the old house and I remember, too, that whenever we came back after a tour there would be a little jar of flowers or leaves on the table to welcome us.

Work now began in earnest. John Ringham had also come to join the company. It was decided it would be best if we called him Johnny to distinguish him from John. It was mid-season and everyone had to spend part of their Christmas holiday initiating us into the parts, dances and stage-management we were to take over. Some other parts had been switched round and minor alterations had to be made to costumes. We had to concentrate mainly on *Dr. Knock* and *The Pardoner's Tale*.

We began with a proper 'read-through', sitting round the fire. What a relief that was after the cue scripts and sketchy rehearsals at Blackburn! After we had ironed out any problems in the scripts, we moved into the rehearsal room. This was a large room with bare floor-boards, heated by a smelly Tortoise stove and lighted by two sets of french windows which opened on to the south-facing terraces in front of the house. Here we rehearsed the plays and roughed out the set and lighting changes. Here Anne taught us the dances and mimes she had created to the music John brought back from his sporadic trips to London. Here John painted when the company were not rehearsing and here we all took part in vigorous movement exercises each day to keep us limbered up and in full command of our bodies.

After a short break for Christmas (during which I learnt my lines) we reassembled at The Warren. I was baffled by all the stage-management tasks. We were never idle. If we were off-stage we were either doing a quick change or a lighting change — on the prompt or music. The scene changes had to be quick and silent and were choreographed like dances. I had to move counter-weights made of bricks roped together, shift screens, throw painted drapes over, change 'jellies' and open 'tabs'. I struggled to move dimmers smoothly, and learn cues for the complicated lighting plots, on our travelling switchboard. It all seemed a far cry from the talks we had been given at Central by the man from Strand Electric!

Somehow it all got done. The first few performances were near at hand (Crickhowell, Abergavenny ?) and we returned to The Warren to sleep. On 12 January I wrote to my parents, 'Many thanks for the parcels. I've received all three safely, the last being cleaning *etc*. It's very late so I won't write much as we have an early start tomorrow and have 274 miles to go. This address is always safe for things to be forwarded. Otherwise P.T.O. (a list of addresses on tour). Lots of love — don't expect many letters. Look after yourselves — Armine.' The first address was Mrs J.B.Pennyman, Ormesby Hall, Ormesby, Nr. Middlesbrough, Yorks.

It was late when we arrived at Ormesby. I can dimly remember standing in the square, pillared hall surrounded by baggage and being welcomed by Colonel and Mrs Pennyman. This time I was not staying at the Hall itself but with the Estate Manager, Tony Elsdon and wife, Pat. However, I joined the others for meals. We spent three nights at Ormesby, playing nearby, and then set out further afield to give a series of performances in schools and town halls.

Ten days after leaving The Warren I woke up in a small hotel in Thirsk. It was my 21st birthday. There were no presents or cards from my family or friends at home and, although the others in the company did their best, it all felt rather flat. Maurice asked me what I would like as a present. 'What I'd really like is a bunch of daffodils.' 'Are you sure?' 'Yes — please.' My father always gave my mother daffodils on my birthday. I suppose I felt it would be a link with home. He disappeared and came back, after a little while, with a small bunch. Johnny saw them and asked where they came from. 'Maurice gave them to me.' 'My dear girl — do you know what they COST?!!' I didn't — but I guessed they were expensive. Now I felt guilty. Perhaps they'd cost as much as 5/-, that would have been one third of our weekly wage. But they lasted a long time and gave me such a lot of pleasure.

We were due back at Ormesby that night. As I was still staying with Tony and Pat (Elsden) and it was extremely late, I rushed to their house. There was a huge collection of cards and birthday presents in my room and when they discovered that it was my 21st birthday they opened a bottle of champagne cider. The next day was Sunday, and Mrs Pennyman's cook made a splendid birthday cake which we all ate together sitting round a blazing log fire in the drawing room.

Ormesby Hall was one of our favourite places. It is a plain Palladian style house built in the first half of the 18th century and we were invited to stay there on several occasions during my time with Compass. It became our base for playing in the area, Saltburn, Whitby, *etc.* and I remember Colonel Pennyman waiting up to give us hot soup in the large warm kitchen when we came back late. Mrs Pennyman was passionately fond of all 'theatre' and under her patronage several small companies stayed at the Hall and played locally. Theatre Workshop had been based there at one time and I believe she also invited The Compass Players to make it their permanent home. In addition, she produced plays herself in the gardens and was well known for her 'innovative theatrical activities'.

As there were not many of us we were privileged to sleep in the house itself and not in the service wing. I remember the young maid who tapped on the door of my four-poster bedroom bringing a cup of early-morning tea and opening the shutters, 'Good morning, Miss. It's 7.30. Breakfast will be at 8.15.' I remember, too, the splendid Victorian bathroom. The huge bath was encased in mahogany and so was the loo, which had one of those brass handles to pull up.

Downstairs in the dining room the table by the window was laid with cereals, eggs and bacon and sometimes herrings in oatmeal. If we were there for an evening meal we sat facing each other (and the family portraits) along the sides of the long, polished table. The Colonel, a staunch Conservative, sat at one end with his back to the window — Mrs Pennyman, who had quite opposite political opinions, sat at the other. She often tried to draw us into discussions and once she asked us what our political views were. When she came to me I faltered, 'I don't know.' 'Liberal!' she announced firmly and passed me over.

I remember how the Colonel sometimes 'laced' our soup with sherry. I also remember how, one afternoon, he and Maurice carried me, struggling, up the main staircase and dumped me on my four-poster bed with strict instructions not to come down until tea-time. I had done masses of wardrobe washing, the chance of hot water and the drying racks high up in the ceiling of the 'Flower Room' was not to be missed. I don't think I was feeling very well and they decided I needed a rest! Everyone was so kind and we met similar kindness many many times on our travels.

I stayed with doctors and lawyers, teachers, caretakers, miners' widows, school friends, relations and friends of my parents. I even stayed with Pam's parents when we played near Congleton and with my own in Exeter. I remember sleeping in little grey Cotswold cottages and larger stone houses in Hutton-le-Hole and Thornton-le-Dale in Yorkshire (where I discovered by chance my hostess was a distant relation). There were, too, rambling Victorian houses such as The Limes at Hinckley where the wonderful Tomkins family always greeted us with open arms and hugged us when we left. They shared with us their food, their rooms and even their corridors when we were fog-bound (various members of the Company slept on mattresses on the floors). In later years they shared their house with the Century Theatre wardrobe.

Many of these generous people were complete strangers and welcomed me into their homes on a first visit in a most trusting manner considering we were strolling players and classed with rogues and vagabonds! On return visits I usually stayed with the same families, sometimes three or four times, and we became firm friends and kept up with each other for many years. 'Do you really all travel in that van?' 'How do you learn all your lines?' 'Do you ever get them mixed up? Find yourself in the wrong play?' 'Where do you rehearse?' 'Do you really make yourselves up?', *etc*. However tired we were we had to stifle our yawns and answer their queries. We also made a special point of writing our 'thank you' letters after each stay. Sometimes, when I mentioned I was Wardrobe Mistress I would be asked, 'How do you manage for material?' I used to explain and add that people occasionally gave us old evening dresses or curtains they didn't want; anything would be gratefully received! I remember when we were playing at Shrewsbury School my hostess, the wife of one of the house-masters, presented us with two beautiful Victorian ball gowns. She recognised my name as being the same as an eccentric old lady who was her cousin as well as mine. I went to see this Armine Sandford while we were there (she was so tiny she walked under my arm when I held the door open for her) and she remarked that she could have played my part as Helen of Troy without there being a change in the programme. She was almost a hundred years old at that time!

We also had an unofficial rating system; sharing a bed ranked low for most of us. We always had clean sheets but to be offered a sherry, a bath and to have biscuits by the bed was in the top rank! I remember an elderly cousin of my mother's who even put sticks of liquorice on the bedside table! I remember, too, kind hosts at Marple, teachers, who had a complete wall of their living room fitted from floor to ceiling with bookshelves packed with colourful Penguins, and other teachers in Warrington who had a small picture of a queue at a chip shop on one wall. They told me that it was by a friend of theirs and that, as he had forgotten to paint a dog in, they had asked him specially to do so. His name, of course, was Lowry, but it was new to me then!

Pam and I often shared 'hospitality' and occasionally a double bed (not so popular!), sometimes we even shared the bath water! I remember a splendid old-fashioned bathroom at Redmire (where our hostess had been several things, including a ballet dancer and a racing driver). Here Pam most unselfishly let me have the water first as I was covered in wet-white (after playing Dynameme) and she was brown (after Doto). She was long-suffering about this on several other occasions! It wouldn't really have mattered, of course, but it was more aesthetically pleasing to get into bath-water resembling milk rather than mud.

Wardrobe on Tour.

In those days all the costumes travelled packed tightly into skips, so that after unloading the van I had to spend a lot of time pressing out the creases as well as cleaning off greasepaint stains from the previous performance. Over the years I used dozens of bottles of Beaucaire at 1/3d a bottle! If I could, I bought C.T.C. from a chemist which was cheaper. Many of the costumes were made of wool, which didn't crumple too badly, but the women's dresses had to be ironed all over. Some months later, rails were added behind the old bus seats on which we sat in the van. This meant that most of the costumes could travel on their hangers and, although it was a bit tricky getting the longer garments in and out of the van *over* the seats — and they got a bit damp if it was raining —, they didn't get so squashed and it saved a lot of time.

I found it bewildering, at first, trying to remember which items of costume to place on each actor's chair (they had to be in just the right order for quick changes) or exactly where to hang them (for the same reason). I also got in a terrible muddle with the make-up kits which also had to be in a certain order around the table. This was more for personal reasons. The actors had already evolved a seating arrangement and liked to have the same neighbours at each performance! Pam helped me to sort things out — in between preparing high tea. We each kept our own collection of grease paints and there was quite a collection of containers (cigar boxes, tins and cash boxes) and, after a few days, I learned who owned which.

We couldn't do without Leichner grease paint, but, to economise, we didn't use their remover or powder. Trex or liquid paraffin and tins of French chalk did just as well. We needed cotton wool but, instead of tissues, I used to go to a chemist and buy rolls of cellulose wadding. (I haven't seen any for ages.) This I cut into squares and peeled the layers apart. It was a bit scratchy but did the job. Also, in the centre of the table was spirit gum and remover, if needed, for beards and moustaches.

If we had to be healthily tanned we coated our limbs in a mixture of Armenian Bole (bought in powder form by the ounce from a chemist) and water. Likewise, if a delicate skin was indicated, we used zinc oxide, water and a dash of glycerine. It saved a lot of money and I don't think our skin suffered at all.

We all had to play a variety of parts and often found ourselves having to 'age' by an incredible number of years. Somewhere I acquired a fine, firm sable-hair paintbrush (which was invaluable for high-lighting wrinkles) together with a dried and pickled rabbit's foot for powdering round the eyes.

Later, at our one day drama schools, I sometimes demonstrated different ways of making up — starting with the simple but effective witch-like 'houri' make-up for *The Pardoner's Tale* (off-white face, green slanting eyeshadow, very heavy black eyebrows and eye lining) and gradually 'ageing' myself — talking and explaining all the time. I think it was quite a useful exercise for members of the audience, many of whom relied on someone else to make them up for performances by their amateur dramatic societies.

Dressing rooms were often a problem, sometimes far from the stage up (or down) stairs. The most uncomfortable dressing rooms we encountered were at Stanley in Co. Durham, where the girls dressed in the ladies' cloakroom on one side of the stage (the lines of coat-hooks kept catching in our hair) and the boys in the men's urinal on the other! I remember too the beautifully patterned lavatories in some of the nether regions of the older parish halls. They were decorated with roses and trailing vines, acanthus leaves and willow pattern and had names like The Cascade, The Royal and The Silent (which seldom was!). I hope some have been rescued for posterity as examples of gracious living!

As far as I was concerned, the main worry on tour was keeping the costumes clean. Some items, (usually white, like shirts and collars), didn't respond to *dry* cleaning (a rubbing with CTC) and needed the old-fashioned soap (or detergent) and water treatment to get rid of the grease paint. In spite of the old maxim, 'It won't show from the front,' we were very particular about the appearance of costumes. I was not always successful. Fuel rationing was still in force and we couldn't rely on hot water and drying facilities. This applied to ourselves and our personal washing as well as the wardrobe!

The men's tights in *The Pardoner's Tale* were an especial headache. They were made of cotton (no Lycra in those days!) and sagged at the knees after only one wearing. The actors did their best to get rid of the wrinkles by tying tapes around pennies (old size) and pulling these tight but even this didn't work after three performances. What a relief it was to stay in a Government hostel or big school, or with a sympathetic hostess who didn't object to her kitchen being festooned with wet garments!

I could normally cope with the high collars for *Box and Cox* while preparing for the show. These came up to the ears and were as hard as cardboard. I usually managed to cover the marks from the first performance by smearing them over with white greasepaint and powder, but this made them all the more difficult to remove, and then it was imperative to wash them. When they were dipped in water they became soft and slimy, but a fierce detergent called 'Tide' (definitely *not* good for my hands) worked wonders. After they had regained their 'whiteness' they were soaked in 'starch' (containing about three times the normal amount of powder) and ironed dry to regain the required stiffness. They must have been very uncomfortable to wear. Once I had an urgent need to replace a pair of white stockings worn in *Time's Fool*. I scoured all the shops in the town ending up, eventually, in a small old-fashioned haberdashers where I was presented with a pair of 'laying-out' stockings.

Sometimes, of course, there were 'running repairs'. Most of these were when stitches came undone with the strain of dancing or quick changes. As a result of this I learned that in the *making* of costumes the size of stitches was immaterial, they could seldom be seen from the front. What did matter was strong seams firmly anchored at both ends and good 'finishing off' for hooks, eyes and other fasteners!

On tour, and at The Warren, I found I was too busy to keep a journal (which is a pity) but I did keep a notebook diary for expenses, and, occasionally, useful addresses, either organisers or Theatrical Costumiers.

I didn't smoke and used very little make-up off stage so my personal expenses consisted mainly of buying my sweet ration — or books. I was often tempted by Boots library books withdrawn from stock. In fact I sometimes didn't use all my 15/- a week 'wages' and collected a lump sum at the end of the tour. Necessary expenses ranged from Beaucaire, greasepaint and mending tape for the wardrobe to lunches, toothpaste and cough sweets for myself.

I seem to have used a lot of Beaucaire, and, on occasions, consumed a quantity of cough sweets! If we had colds or coughs we could seldom go to bed and kept going on Meggazones and a strong cough linctus, Syrup of Cosillana. I remember once we had to help Maurice on stage for a matinée of *Comus*. He was decidedly 'woozy'. Perhaps he was suffering from an overdose!

During rehearsals for *A Phoenix Too Frequent*, we spent a few blissful days at John and Bettina Headley's beautiful old half-timbered house at Forstal in Kent. We rehearsed in a barn and I remember the sunshine and tulips in the garden, the woods a sea of bluebells and the nightingales singing! My skills as Wardrobe Mistress were not taxed too much for the double bill. The costumes for *Tinker's Wedding* were adapted from clothes John chose from the existing wardrobe with the addition of the black and green wool 'ironing blanket' which doubled as a shawl for the old woman (a marvellous performance by Moira). It had a number of scorch marks and blotches which gave extra character, as did the faint smell of burning! This blanket returned to the stage, again as a shawl, for *Strange Return* in 1951.

Of Gods and Men supplied the costumes for *A Phoenix Too Frequent*. As Dynamane I wore the long white chiton and emerald-green cloak bordered with silver leaves (made from barrage balloon material) which had been Persephone's; Martin, as Tegeus, wore a tunic and cloak which had, I believe, belonged to two different characters (these only needed minor additions to make them into a uniform).

The first night of the two plays was in Workington to an appreciative audience who laughed in all the right places. We had been concentrating so much on the emotions in later rehearsals I had forgotten how funny *Phoenix* was. On tour, the weather was sunny and the village halls became extremely hot by the end of the evening. I remember I got very thirsty (there are a lot of words in *Phoenix*), and quite looked forward to the drink of 'wine' (diluted Camp Coffee, gravy browning or cold tea, tasting of varnish) from the pottery bowls made by Lew at Taena and beautifully decorated by John with Greek designs. Martin, who off-stage was rather pale and wore glasses, looked very handsome as the tanned Tegeus (although I remember when once he had a streaming cold and addressed me: 'Dydabede, Dydabede, I love you Dydabede' — poor Martin! It wasn't easy for either of us to feel very romantic in those circumstances.

After the summer tour we returned to The Warren for a more intensive rehearsal period. It was then that my real challenge as 'Wardrobe Mistress' began.

Soon after I joined the company John had taken me up the steep flight of stairs which led from the landing and, passing a cosy little room which was used as a bedroom, we had turned left into the first wardrobe attic. It was not very large and had thick oak rafters — so hard with age that it was virtually impossible to drive a nail into them to hang things on. There was a tiny north-facing window lighting a small space and a way through to a door on the far side. The room was crammed with skips, old suitcases and cardboard boxes of every shape and size piled high against the walls. These were filled with a miscellaneous collection of hats, gloves, boots and shoes; buttons, buckles and belts; ribbons, pieces of lace, Victorian trimmings, old curtains and odd lengths of material; shawls and scarves. There were feathers and fans, and fans made of feathers, I remember especially a beautiful white one made of ostrich feathers, the sort 'debs' carried when they were presented at court (I always hoped we could use it but it was never suitable). There were 'props' of one sort or another and carpet-bags and hold-alls. The skips were packed tight with a motley assortment of costumes; as far as possible the ones from past productions were kept together but as it was so often necessary to re-use them these were invariably mixed up. John knew roughly where things were but it often took ages to unearth a specific garment, especially if he sent me to look for it and I had only his description to go on, having never seen it before. I never found out where all the things had come from, I assume a great number had been donated from other people's attics as 'coming in useful for theatricals'. John would sometimes say, 'That came from so-and-so,' or, 'That was my mother's.' I don't know how we could have managed without this 'stock'.

At some time during my first spring with the company, John fixed long rails in the second, larger attic which stretched above his and Anne's bedroom. The ceilings were so low he'd had to stoop all the time, but he had hung most of the costumes on hangers so that it was now possible to walk along and see at a glance what was available. (Inevitably, smaller items like shoes and shirts had to remain in boxes.) This was a tremendous advantage in future productions and saved a lot of time.

One of my first jobs during the summer rehearsal period was to help sort the costumes into groups:— Victorian, Greek, Timeless, Mediaeval-style gowns and long cloaks *etc.* I then had to give them a dusting with an anti-moth powder — D.D.T. The attic already had a musty smell but after *our* efforts it was almost impossible to breathe up there, especially in hot weather. The smell wore off a little, in time, and the powder was certainly effective. We didn't know then how dangerous it was to human beings as well as to moths.

As each production came and went, the number of costumes in the attic grew. Members of the company also contributed garments of diverse sorts. I don't remember that we ever had to hire a costume though, undoubtedly, we occasionally borrowed. It was always John's dream that the member companies of the Union of Independent Theatres (The Compass Players, the Century Theatre and the Adelphi Guild Theatre) should share their wardrobes so that costumes could be borrowed from stock and thus save a great deal of time, effort and money. Unfortunately this was not to be — though when the Adelphis folded we did, I believe, inherit most, if not all, of their wardrobe. We certainly borrowed their costumes for *Comus*.

The other main wardrobe area at The Warren was the workroom where the costumes were actually made. It was a large, light airy room with two long windows looking west over some rhododendron bushes to the wood along the ridge behind the house and farm. In hot weather we were able to open these windows and sit on the little patch of grass outside to sew on buttons and trimmings. The treadle sewing machine stood in front of one window to get maximum light and, after an initial period of acute frustration trying to thread the unusually shaped shuttle, I found I could manage quite well, with a bit of practice. I had used my mother's old hand-powered machine during the war and was accustomed to 'make do and mend' sewing. (Once, though, I stitched right through the middle finger of my left hand. It poured blood but didn't hurt much — it was Maurice who nearly fainted when I asked him to put a plaster on for me!)

The costumes for the productions were obtained in several ways:
1. *Specially designed* by John and made from new material.
2. From *stock* which consisted of:
   a) oddments acquired over the years, *e.g.* Victorian frock coats, bodices, cassocks, old curtains, *etc.*
   b) costumes originally specially designed for past productions and now relegated to the attic, *e.g. The Quest* and *Of Gods and Men.*
3. A *mixture* of both.
4. *Borrowed*, e.g. *Comus.*
5. *Bought* tights, stockings, some shoes, *etc.*
6. *Donated* by members of the company or people on tour.
7. I think we may have *hired* swords.

Clothes rationing was in force but certain materials, such as black-out material, were not on coupons. I don't think felt was either, but it was expensive.

Comus was, I think, the first production we worked on that summer. The strikingly beautiful black and white costumes were by the distinguished designer, T. Osborne Robinson. They arrived in a skip from Macclesfield all mixed up, but luckily we had Tom's designs so we were able to sort out how the pieces fitted together. Some garments had to be replaced as they had been lost or didn't fit the new wearers and they all needed refurbishing to a certain extent. Tom's drawings were somewhat distorted so it was sometimes difficult to see the exact proportions (where elbows and knees came, for example). If in doubt it was always possible to ask John's advice although I had to be careful to choose the right moment. He could be somewhat irascible if interrupted when he was busy. I was not so much afraid of John but of his displeasure!

Tom had dressed *Comus* and his Crew totally in black, the Attendant Spirit predominantly in white and the Humans in a combination of black and white with silver decorations (cut from scrolls of barrage balloon material). The Spirit in disguise as the Shepherd had touches of grey on his smock and Sabrina, Goddess of the River, wore a flowing dress (made from a damask table cloth) with a long train embellished with waves (of barrage balloon again), which swished as she moved. Tom had used felt and net in many of the costumes. The Lady's skirt was made with yards of curtain net.

The two Brothers wore hats, into which were stitched wigs made from sisal (made in our workshops, not borrowed). We had, too, to make new masks for Comus's retainers, known to us as the 'Ugly Bugglies'. These were of stiff buckram, painted black, and went right over our heads and necks. These packed flat for travelling and were shaped like snouts. They were horribly hot to dance in and, although we pricked holes over our eyes hoping we could see out, we found this almost impossible on the dimly lit stage and could really only see a small patch of floor beneath our chins. Martin (doubling with the first Brother) once danced right off a low stage during a schools matinee and straight back on again without a pause — to the astonishment of the front row.

The setting was very simple, screens (with painted 'headers') and a central opening with a rostrum and a silver wooden throne which took to pieces for travelling. The Brothers carried swords which were used for a mime; the shepherd a crook; the Spirit a long silver branched wand. The only other prop I remember was a huge silver goblet (carved from a solid piece of wood) in which Comus offered wine to the Lady to tempt her from the path of virtue.

This production with its original music and songs and lit by John with great imagination (as always) attracted a great deal of favourable comment. I remember in particular an article in the *Times Educational Supplement* and also one Schools Inspector who confessed, after seeing a matinée (at Bishop Auckland?), that he had come thinking we could never hold the children's attention with a Masque such as this, and how pleasantly surprised he had been.

The other production that summer was *All For Truth*, Molière's *Le Misanthrope*, brilliantly translated into rhyming couplets by P.D.Cummins. John had specially designed costumes for this and it was a question of finding suitable materials to match his ideas rather than creating costumes from available bits and pieces. As we were members of The Showman's

Guild we were able to get coupons for petrol. We were also given an allocation of clothing coupons for new productions although I can't remember how many. John would make trips to town and come back with lengths of material and little bits of organza for ruffles and collars. He bought yards of tape and coloured braids (the sort used in schools for games to distinguish different teams) and lots of white silky material called celanese for sleeves and jabots (in my younger days it was used for petticoats before the advent of nylon). He also bought felt and black-out material.

He had, I think, already 'ear-marked' certain materials in the wardrobe stock (pieces of velvet, lace and brocade) which he incorporated into his designs with the new stuffs. When John put his costume designs on paper they were clear in detail and easy to follow, thank goodness. In his paintings the figures were often slightly out of proportion but for his theatre designs (at least in the working drawings) he used a more conventional style so that it was possible to see, for example, if a coat sleeve came to just above the wrist (with a *little* bit of shirt showing) or just below the elbow (with a *lot* of shirt exposed). Sometimes he made little diagrams to show how to create an effect but usually he would explain how to do things as we went along.

His costumes for *All For Truth* conveyed the essence of the period without a lot of fussy detail. On the whole, he used plain materials decorated with braid or tape or with painted designs (on cuffs or waistcoats for example). He did these himself at great speed. The colours were suited to the characters. For instance *Célimène*, the coquette (a part I much enjoyed playing), was dressed in a bright, hard, emerald green taffeta overskirt looped over a black and white striped dress. This was made from black-out material with white strips of horribly slippery celanese, sewn on individually. It took hours but was most effective. *Eliante*, gentle and kind, was in pastel shades, mainly blue. *Alceste* (le Misanthrope himself), terribly sincere, was to wear a dark brown coat. We must have run out of coupons (or money) and we had no suitable material, so John removed a length of the old bottle-green serge curtains which hung from a long pole in the hall and which we pulled on winter nights to keep out the draughts. They were probably Victorian, and it was a bit like the Tara episode in *Gone With the Wind*. He assured me that, boiled in orange dye, this would turn a rich brown and, in spite of sceptical remarks from some of the company, he was right. (The coat, with different facings and cuffs and worn over another waistcoat was used again for Mr Fussy in *Time's Fool*.) *Arsinoë* should have been dressed in a hard bright yellow skirt draped with black lace (an old evening dress) to suit her waspish nature. John had not been able to find the acid yellow cloth he wanted and presented me with a length of primrose-coloured rayon and some deep yellow dye. I spent the whole of a very hot afternoon sweating over a pan of steaming liquid, heated by our temperamental primus stove outside the kitchen, but the rayon refused to change colour. At last I had to go to John and admit defeat. I think it was the only case of John's design not being achieved by the finished costume.

In time, all the costumes were completed. We were working under constant pressure as there was a lot of stitching to do and virtually all the costumes were made from scratch. We were greatly helped by a number of friends who came from far and wide to sew, stitch and create (not only costumes but props and scenery as well). Most of these were members of the Adelphi companies but I remember also a friend of Maurice's called Susie from America who, amazed that we had not heard the songs from *South Pacific*, regaled us with, 'I'm gonna wash that man right out of my hair', and 'I'm in love with a wonderful guy'.

But, above all, we were indebted to George Ineson's wife, Connie. We could not have managed without her. She was a professional dressmaker and knew how to cut cloth. John would make her a few sketches and after a brief consultation she would take an actor's measurements and with the aid of a few pins, a tape-measure and sharp scissors she would cut out bodices, sleeves, cuffs and coats without a pattern. I was filled with admiration. The costumes always hung beautifully and fitted well. The rest of us could do simple sewing, stitch things together and adapt, but, even though I was officially Wardrobe Mistress, I could never have attempted the major work.

One of the difficulties of making costumes at The Warren was that we could not use electric irons, which would not work on the Direct Current system. We had to learn to put flat irons into the Aga oven and judge when they were the right temperature to press the various materials (quite a knack!). I never quite mastered the traditional method of spitting on them and, after the first few experiences of scorching, I always tested them first on an odd scrap of cloth. There was also the risk of burning ourselves, either on the irons or on the Aga. It was a great relief to get out on tour and be able to use the electric iron again with its temperature control and insulated handle.

Wigs and Hair

The wigs for *All For Truth* were, as far I remember, made mainly in the kitchen. The cost of hiring or buying five full-bottomed wigs would have been prohibitive and this posed a major problem until Johnny had the ingenious idea of making them from sisal.

I think the method was as follows: long lengths of fibre were cut and the strands laboriously teased apart. The crinkly bits were soaked in water, ironed straight and then dyed the appropriate colour. After this they were stitched on to wig bases purchased from a professional wigmaker. Moira, who had, I believe, had training as a hairdresser, then cut them to shape and curled them into ringlets with tongs. The resulting wigs were heavy and rather clumsy but blended in well with John's beautifully simplified versions of the 17th-century costumes. They were credited to 'John Henry' (Johnny Ringham's two Christian names) and 'Bert' in the programme!

After this, dyed sisal was used whenever wigs were needed, often stitched into hats to facilitate quick changes. We did, though, for some productions, also use professionally made wigs, for example Maurice's tonsure as the Monk/Mephistophelis in *Dr Faustus* and in *Time's Fool* where Mr Fussy was portrayed as wearing a wig to cover his bald head (I shall never forget the audience's reaction which followed the hilarious 'business' when his stringy grey wig was whisked off to reveal a shiny pate underneath. School children in particular laughed so much they almost literally fell off their chairs. It virtually stopped the show!).

Where it was necessary to use false beards and moustaches, these too were professionally made. The girls wore their own hair, curled into ringlets when needed. Grey-haired wigs for character parts would have been too expensive so we had to cover our hair with powder and streaks of greasepaint which looked reasonable but was a problem if we had difficulty in getting hot water on tour to wash it out again.

Tights, stockings and footwear

I don't remember clearly how we obtained tights and stockings. I suppose we wrote off to London to a theatrical costumier sending details of sizes and appropriate numbers of coupons. They were only supplied, I think, in black or white so we had to dye them to get the required colour. As they were made of pure cotton they took dye well.

For the mediaeval costumes and *Comus*, leather soles were stitched on to the feet of tights, a slow and painful business as the leather was stiff and it was hard work, and awkward, pushing a needle through with one hand inside the foot. We frequently pricked our fingers.

We danced mostly in ballet shoes or bare feet. In *All For Truth* and *Time's Fool* the girls wore 'character' shoes and the men ordinary leather shoes (sometimes covered in felt) with the heels reddened and buckles added. The felt was stuck on with a white milky glue called, I think, 'cow-gum', later to be replaced by Copydex. If it spilled or spread one could rub it off when dry except off felt, so we had to be rather careful. Boots and sandals were worn when appropriate.

Props and more costumes

In *All For Truth* the girls carried fans. There were some beautiful fans in the attic, some were hand-painted and perhaps should have been in a museum. As Célimène I used a lovely little white silk one painted with black flowers, which might have been designed to go with my dress.

There were few other props:— a letter, a poem, a candlestick, two specially designed chairs and a table (with hinged legs so that they could be folded for travelling). The curtains for the window and central back archway were made in the workroom and John painted 'headers' to go on top of the screens and charming plaques (depicting flowers and musical instruments) to hang upon them.

The first night of *All For Truth* was at a Government hostel in Malvern. I was so glad to get there! It had been a gloriously hot summer but the water at The Warren had almost dried up. I remember queuing up for a few inches of bath water (after Anne and Lizzie) and I had not been able to wash my hair for five weeks.

Later that year, when Moira left to return to Ireland, Joyce came to join the company. We replaced *Tinker's Wedding* with *The Proposal*. The costumes were from stock.

The next summer we put in the Shaw double bill — *Village Wooing* and *The Great Catherine*, as a 'light' programme. I was not in *Village Wooing* (which was most skilfully played by Pam and Maurice) but was Catherine in the second play.

Costumes were no great problem for *Village Wooing* and the set was simplicity itself. The ship in the first scene was suggested by two deck chairs and a couple of painted life-belts hung on the screens. I made some cheerful blue and white check gingham curtains for the shop, which were attached to a small false window sandwiched between two screens. Two chairs, a telephone and a canvas 'counter' (propped on a table and painted in perspective illustrating goods for sale) completed the set. Typically, John had included some jokes on the canvas — one being a jar labelled 'Mr Shaw's Ginger Balls'. I don't know if anyone in the audience noticed.

Dr Faustus and *Man Overboard* were our next two major productions. We had been joined by two friends from New Zealand — Collin Hansen and Raymond Parkes — and that meant we could tackle more elaborate productions with more characters — and that meant more costumes.

I don't know how many there were in *Dr Faustus*. Martin (as Faustus) was on stage all the time, Maurice (as Mephistophelis) most of the time (although he also doubled as Pride), the rest of us played anything from three to six parts each — and that didn't include the complicated stage-management. I think there were about 36 characters in total. In many instances, John had transformed scenes with speaking parts into mimes (brilliantly choreographed by Anne) but these still needed costumes. I seemed to spend most of my waking hours stitching away — as usual with many helpers. I especially remember Phoebe Waterfield, who had great experience of wardrobe with the Adelphis, sitting up late with me.

It was now that the rails John had put in the attic really proved their worth. He was able to walk along taking a top here, a tunic there and a cloak from somewhere else, all of which he combined to make an homogeneous whole. His unerring sense of colour made this a fairly quick operation and I would come down from the attic with armfuls of bits of costumes.

However, as the finished creations were in his 'mind's-eye' (there were no sketches) the actual making of the new costumes was not so easy. I frequently had to pluck up courage to ask, 'John, did you mean this piece to go here or here?' Often the only way was to get the actor to stand as a model and drape the oddments on him, pinning things to John's direction.

I remember that as Envy I wore an assortment of greens: lime-green tights and a dark green woolly top covered with a 1930s-style green and white dress which John (rather to my alarm) tore and slashed on me with scissors to give a ragged appearance. Wrath wore an amalgamation of five different red and orange garments which clashed horribly and gave a really angry effect. The Pope's costume was made from an old sheet, and on his gloved hand he wore a large red ring — a bicycle reflector! Everything had to be firmly stitched together with easy fastenings for quick changes.

One of the most beautiful costumes needed no alteration. Pam had given a lovely pure white silk chiffon dress to the wardrobe and John now chose it for Helen of Troy. It was perfect — made in the Greek style with masses of tiny pleats. It rippled gently as I moved very, very slowly (to give the impression of floating) across the raised rostrum at the back of the stage against a deep blue cyc and highlighted by a lavender spot. Although I couldn't see the effect myself I could almost feel the audience holding its breath. It must have been a magical theatrical moment — especially with the emotional Richard Strauss music adding an extra dimension.

Masks and Mumming

My first experience of wearing masks was in *The Pardoner's Tale* (where the Constable and Shopkeepers wore half-masks and the Old Man — who was Death — wore a full one). This enabled us to double most effectively without changes of make-up, though I used to have fun as the Vintner, making my chin up to match my mask. John also used half-masks, but in the Commedia dell'Arte style, for the two clerks in *Time's Fool*.

It was, however, the masks for *Dr Faustus* which were so inspired. John, of course, made all the moulds — tailored to fit the actors' faces. During the rehearsal period every available person could be seen busily pasting on little strips of paper. When dry, the resulting masks were painted by John and then hung around the house, mainly in the living room, to be kept out of harm's way (some bore an uncanny resemblance to their wearers!) There were beautiful masks in gold and silver for the Spirits; horribly decomposing faces to convey the corruption of the Pope's court; the more straightforward masks for Darius, Alexander and his Paramour; a variety of devils; a hideous old woman; an old man (re-used from *The Pardoner's Tale*) and, of course, the remarkable Seven Deadly Sins.

We in the wardrobe did not help make the papier-mâché for the masks themselves but we did help make the head-dresses. Many of these were constructed of wire covered in hessian and painted by John. Some were attached to the masks themselves but mostly they were sewn on to hoods which went over the head and neck. There was even a pair of antlers. As for the Sins: *Pride* wore a velvet hat with grand feathers; *Wrath* had spikey red sisal hair sewn onto a scarlet hood; a large spider sat on top of *Sloth's* head; hollow-eyed *Covetousness* had grasping hands (made from old gloves stuffed with rags); painted green snakes made from thick wire coiled round *Envy's* head; and pig-faced *Gluttony* wore a wimple. Joyce's own hair was visible behind the mask for *Lechery* whose face was deadly pale — one eye closed in a lascivious wink. For the other, John had used a huge amber glass eye which had fallen out of a rather battered leopard skin I had once brought back from Exeter. Most of the masks fitted well, though they were inevitably hot and stuffy, and my mask as Envy was so twisted I found it difficult to see out of the lop-sided eyes. On tour, these masks travelled in a skip of their own.

There were a number of props for *Dr Faustus* — the largest (and most dramatic perhaps) an 'orrery' of looped metal — we called it the astrolabe — which John lit from below to create fantastic shadow effects. There were precious gifts for the Spirits to offer Faustus, including a length of gold and silver brocade from the attic, and books. Off-stage on opposite sides, we carefully placed a large empty biscuit tin and an ancient gramophone horn. The Evil Angel spoke across the first and the Good Angel spoke through the second. They produced a suitably unearthly effect. By the time the costumes of *Dr Faustus* were completed I knew the wardrobe attic intimately and could even, on occasions, suggest garments for John to use.

For *Man Overboard* John followed the usual pattern of creating costumes from new material and stock in the attic. I also remember bringing some genuine Middle Eastern bits and pieces from home which came in handy. On the whole, the Biblical garments were fairly straightforward to make and, although there was a lot of sewing, I can't remember it being such a marathon as *Dr. Faustus*. There were, however, the costumes for the huge fish — some of John's most unusual designs. The vain Goldfish (Pam), the placid Plaice (Joyce), the aggressive Swordfish (Hedley) and the politically motivated Red Herring (me) were all trapped in their own equivalent of Hell — the belly of the whale. The hessian costumes were made like enormous paper bags (cut to the appropriate shape) on to which John painted scales, fins, eyes and gills.

John's version of *Den Stundenlöse* (under his pen-name Adam Angus) was the next major production as far as wardrobe was concerned. After a lot of deliberation at company meetings we called it *Time's Fool*. It was a delicious comedy and I remember a Danish student coming to see us (after a performance at a teacher training college in Durham) to say how delighted he was — and intrigued — to find an English company doing a play by Holberg, a dramatist as well known in Denmark as Molière is in France.

John used many garments from stock (mainly coats and the longer dresses), bringing them into the 18th-century with changes of cuffs, collars and waistcoats. He designed some all-enveloping costumes, decorated with wide bands of black and gold, for the two clerks, who also wore black shovel hats and half-masks to facilitate doubling. For Pernille, the scheming maidservant, he bought some cheeky, red and white striped cotton for the dress, which he combined with a pale grey overskirt (from the attic) and organza ruffles and cuffs. (After Pam left, I took over this part which was tremendous fun to play — a bit like Maria in *Twelfth Night*, a part I also took over from Pam some years later with the Century Theatre!)

Another dress which I remember especially was the one I originally wore in *Time's Fool* as Mr Fussy's daughter Leonora. It was the most lovely Victorian white silk-brocade ball gown and had been given to us (together with another antique dress) by my hostess in Shrewsbury some years before. John altered the style of the neckline and sleeves (I carefully avoided cutting the material) and added a delicate swathe of tiny pink rosebuds which he showed me how to make from curled strips of pink cotton. It made a splendid wedding dress. I suppose it should really have gone to a museum but we were desperate for any material we could get. It was a case of necessity not being a virtue! I can't remember any panics at the dress rehearsal, but I noted in my diary for 1 July 1951, '4 a.m. bed!!'

On 14 July 1951 we took part in the very special quincentenary celebrations at Northleach in the Cotswolds. The whole village 'went mediaeval' for the day, the chemist's shop became the Apothecary's and the Baker's window was full of home-baked cottage loaves. We were The Strolling Players, and took over the role of a Guild, performing an Ancient Mumming Play in the Square in the afternoon and The Wakefield Shepherd's Play 'outside John Fortey's house' at 7 o'clock. We spent the whole day in mediaeval costume with the rest of the villagers. For *Mac the Sheep Stealer* we acted on a cart which raised us above our audience, most of whom had never seen anything like this before and enjoyed the simple humour of the shepherds. It was a fairly light summer evening but there was no sun, although it hadn't yet set. I was playing Mary the Mother of God in the scene where the shepherds bring presents to the baby Jesus. As I moved forward holding the bundle representing the child I had a line resembling 'God who gave us heavenly light', and suddenly the sun came from behind a cloud and I was bathed in a shaft of sunlight. Later in the pub two old men were heard chatting over a pint and discussing the play — one turned to the other and said, 'And when that woman came out with that baby...!! and when that woman came out with that baby...!!' He was so moved he couldn't find the right words to finish the sentence.

Our last production was *Strange Return*, a rather sombre piece in which I was the dishonest, middle-aged stall-keeper, Mme Piquot. It was quite a dramatic part, I remember, and there was one scene where I became hysterical with remorse and fear. The costumes were Victorian and adapted from stock. There was a certain amount of alteration but I don't think any great difficulties. It was a play full of symbolism and moral dilemmas but I don't remember much about it except the atmospheric lighting — full of foreboding — and the emotive music of Richard Strauss. The first night was at an Educational Settlement in the Rhondda Valley and I think we had trouble with the set.

I always loved going back to The Warren at the end of a tour. The branches swished along the roof of the van as we bumped up the drive (Pam always used to say it was the tree spirits welcoming us home) and there were warm greetings from the members of the company who had remained behind. John sometimes visited us on tour to give notes and occasionally to act with us but on the whole in my time he, Anne and later Joyce stayed at The Warren with the growing number of little girls. It was good to see them again. It was also exciting to see what new pictures John had painted while we were away. He hung them round the house and they glowed on the walls with their swirling, meticulous brush strokes. I remember especially a small picture of a red-robed cardinal walking up an avenue of trees towards a distant, beckoning Christ and The Agony in the Garden — with its spikey, curving, green-blue foliage. In his religious pictures John always seemed to paint the face of Christ to look like his own. I was very fond of a picture which I think was there when I joined the company, of Pierrot, seated in the foreground, plucking off the petals of a flower while Columbine and Harlequin danced off together behind him. Once he asked me in to model for him. He needed a detail in the fingers of the woman in *Genesis*. I remember so clearly standing with my arms raised while he painted. It gave me a strange thrill to see the picture again at the posthumous exhibition in Westminster Cathedral. And so many others too, which had been part of my life at The Warren. It was like meeting old friends again.

I remember also how John used to show us the new brochures and programmes for the coming season when they arrived from the printers. As with everything else, John always paid strict attention to detail, and the clear design and distinguished type on good quality paper were intended to create a good first impression on everyone who received the former through the post or bought the latter at performances. I'm sure they did. All these years later it still gives me pleasure to hold them in my hand — not so much a question of 'feel the width' but 'feel the quality'! Just occasionally, if I had no wardrobe tasks to do, I would help Maurice stick on stamps or address envelopes for sending out the publicity.

In addition to being a fine and versatile actor, Maurice was a most efficient company manager. He also arranged the tours, before Gerard Heller joined the company and became our official tours manager. On tour, Maurice took charge of the day-to-day running of the company from coping with finances and dealing tactfully with organisers and hotel proprietors to driving the van and, as far as possible, arranging that we should spend our rare days off in pleasant surroundings. We turned to him for advice on all manner of subjects and I am grateful to him for teaching me so much — both on and off-stage.

Although The Warren was situated in the most lovely countryside, I think most of us were usually too busy to go for long walks — if we did find the time, this made each walk even more special. I remember that twice I walked down past the farm and into the woods beyond and on across fields and gorse where there were hundreds of rabbits (it was not called The Warren for nothing!) to the next estate where there were ponds and canals. On one of these walks, I remember, we found a rabbit in a snare and my brother, who was visiting us, killed it with a blow to put it out of its misery. He was studying medicine and knew where to hit.

Sometimes in the spring, just before supper, I took twenty minutes or so off to clamber up the steep bank behind the house and along a narrow path between the trees to an open space on the ridge from where you could see the Black Mountains in one direction and the Severn Estuary in the other. It was quite magical in bluebell-time. Another favourite short walk was to the end of the drive and back. Marvellous when the rhododendrons were in flower — and the honeysuckle!

I was always very interested to learn about the latest developments at Taena. I never really got to know any members of the Community very well but when they decided to become affiliated to Prinknash Abbey and created the simple little chapel in the old farmhouse I occasionally slipped down to sit in the peaceful white-walled room when Compline was being said. Although I was not a Catholic myself, I found it a very calming experience and I was always welcomed.

Looking back, I realise that the time we actually spent acting was only a small part of our working day. I suppose, when we were tired and under pressure, we did occasionally get 'tetchy' with one another but usually humour prevailed. I remember that, if things were going badly during a set-up, Martin would threaten to put on *The Ride of the Walküre*.

Inevitably, being young and healthy and living and working in close proximity, we fell in and out of love with one another, which led in some cases to personal unhappiness but in another to a permanent relationship — we were all delighted to attend Martin and Joyce's wedding in London one dull November day! But these shared years we spent working together also helped create lasting and affectionate friendships. In times of crisis, such as serious illness, accident or death, we are in constant touch by telephone, passing on the news and giving what support we can.

By the summer of 1951 there had been a lot of changes in the company. Moira had left some time ago to go back to Ireland. Hedley too was gone. Collin and Ray reached the end of their allotted time with us, Joyce was now busy with a baby daughter and Pam also decided to leave. We were joined by a friend of mine from drama school days — Sybil Ewbank — (who was the niece of Dame Sybil Thorndyke and had the same rich voice). John Hoskin, a sculptor from Cheltenham, Anthony Hipwell and his fiancée, Mona Glynn, now completed the acting company.

John produced *Strange Return* but he really wanted to go back to being a painter full-time and told us so. We hoped that the company could carry on with Martin as artistic director and John in the background as adviser. We were doing better than ever before and playing a number of prestigious 'venues' including several large public schools. But by the middle of the autumn tour I was feeling unsettled. I still loved the work, but somehow the chemistry of the company had changed for me and I felt I wanted to try new theatrical experiences and perhaps some broadcasting, television and film work. I wrote to John and Anne to say that, with many regrets, I would like to leave at the end of the spring tour. They were most understanding and wrote a lovely letter back.

Soon after this I wrote to Richard Ward to ask if there was any chance of joining the Century Theatre. We had visited the building site in Hinckley from time to time and watched this extraordinarily brave project grow. After saying, 'It's a superb idea but it won't work,' we had changed our minds when we had seen that it was, after all, going to succeed. I explained to Richard that, more than anything else, I would like to join the company. He wrote back that he was sorry but the cast was already chosen.

Sometime later a company meeting was held at The Warren, I think at Richard's suggestion. He pointed out, gravely, that among other things The Compass Players would not be the same without John and that it would be dishonest to continue functioning under that name. After a great deal of discussion we came to the conclusion, regretfully, that it would be best if the company went into voluntary liquidation. At Easter, 1952, Bertha made her last journey to The Warren and the company dispersed for the last time.

The costumes eventually went to Jay Vernon, Johnny Ringham's 'mentor', a wise and talented producer of amateur drama in Cheltenham. Johnny and Maurice both took their driving tests in Bertha but I don't think she passed her own M.O.T. test and after the last journey had to be sold as scrap.

I think the years I spent with The Compass Players were the most artistically rewarding of my career and I am proud and grateful to have been part of such a very special little company. I am particularly proud of our work in schools. We must have played to thousands of children and I hope some of them remember us and were glad we came. I do know that if I meet people who saw us as adults their eyes light up when they talk about the shows. I don't think the glasses I now wear are too strongly rose-tinted, for I can hold in my hand appreciative criticisms from prestigious national newspapers such as the *Daily Telegraph*, the *Manchester Guardian* and the *News Chronicle* as well as more local publications.

Those years taught me to be resourceful and to adapt to circumstances, to accept challenges and to control an audience. I was able to travel the length and breadth of the country and I met people and visited places I would never otherwise have known. I was given the opportunity to use what talents I possessed to the full and to play some marvellous parts with a group of dedicated people working as a team both on and off stage. We all enjoyed acting together and respected each other and our audiences. All our energies were directed towards giving of our best to the productions as a whole and I don't remember any selfishness of any kind. At the time I joined the company it was, I think. very well-balanced, with the older members — Hedley, Moira and Maurice — adding richer characterisations to the more youthful interpretations of the rest of us. John's personality was so strong that it stamped itself upon us, especially those of us who were young and impressionable, and I think we all recognised that he was a rare and exceptionally talented human being.

It was John's vision and over-all artistic control which gave the company its distinctive style. He moulded us together his way, like a benevolent dictator, so that the company had a unity to which we all contributed our own personalities and performances and this bond created friendships which have lasted to this day. It was a unique and unforgettable experience.

I remember too all these things in no particular order:

The river at Durham being frozen solid one cold January.

A performance of *The Pardoner's Tale* at Canterbury where, during the opening speech by Chaucer (who should have been highlighted by a single spot on an otherwise dark stage) the whole stage was illuminated by two rows of pink electric lights fixed on the side walls of the hall. They would have spoiled all subsequent black-outs! We got them turned off and, when we asked afterwards why they had been on at all, we were told they were the 'morality' (not emergency!) lights.

A magical journey with Bertha's headlights glistening on branches laden with snow, one dark night somewhere in Derbyshire.

The audience muttering all through *All For Truth* at Bettws-y-Coed. We couldn't understand why because they didn't seem bored and applauded loudly. We were told afterwards that the English-speaking members were translating the lines as we spoke them to the Welsh-speaking ones.

When we played at a Government hostel at Holmrook not far from Wastwater, I remember someone telling us that an important project was about to take place in the area. It was still secret. Looking back, I think it was probably the Nuclear Power Station at Windscale.

And a strange experience at Selby Abbey where we were taken into an eerie windowless room high in the thickness of the walls. Our guide said he thought it had been used for Black Mass. It certainly had an unpleasant clammy atmosphere.

There were Alarums

The explosion, which should have coincided with Mephistophelis' entrance in *Dr Faustus*, going off much too soon at a school in Bedford. Shortly afterwards the First Scholar had the line, 'I wonder what's become of Faustus...': singularly apt we thought.

Another time, poor Hedley was taken ill towards the end of *All For Truth* at Wooton-under-Edge. He must have eaten something 'off' at supper. Just after the line, 'Witness my weakness, witness how I bend', he dashed off stage and was violently sick. We paused and started again — again he had to disappear. Finally, we had to bring down the curtain. Maurice explained to the audience what had happened. We had no understudies so we couldn't continue. Looking back, I don't believe he told them the end of the story. John was stupefied when he heard.

Some months later 'flu hit me in the middle of *All For Truth* at Haslingden (Hedley and Pam had already had it and had managed to give even better performances than usual with high temperatures). My legs suddenly turned to water and I had to finish the last act sitting down. By the Friday I had a very nasty cough. I woke in the early hours with a terrible pain in my chest and could hardly breathe — I probably had a touch of pleurisy — but my hostess called in a doctor friend who gave me an injection which resulted in immediate improvement. Perhaps it was my first expereience of penicillin? Anyway, we had a week-end with kind friends in Windermere who nursed us back to some sort of health.

At the Monday set-up in Windermere, however, Hedley fell off a ladder and hurt his hip. He must have been in great pain but played Alceste with the help of a walking stick. My grandmother, who had come over from Ambleside by taxi, said she had 'never seen such a convincing limp'. After the show Hedley was rushed to hospital in Kendal and stayed there about six weeks with a chipped pelvis. Fortunately it was the end of the spring tour.

I remember once at The Warren several of us were in the living room and Johnny went through to light the Tortoise stove for rehearsals. Suddenly, we heard a small, high pitched voice calling, 'Help! Help!' To start with, we thought he was playing the fool, but when the cries persisted we opened the door to find Johnny with his foot over the mouth of a metal jerry-can and the Tortoise surrounded by leaping flames. By mistake, he had tried to light it with petrol instead of paraffin. Somehow we put out the fire before everything exploded. We were all very shaken.

Once we nearly had a catastrophe at a school in Bideford. When we went for lunch in the hall, I switched off the iron (I really did — I proved it later!) and left it on the ironing board we had been loaned — normally I used the old blanket. Someone passing through thought it was still on and flicked the switch the other way. Luckily the smoke was spotted before the fire started.

And Excursions

Occasionally on tour we would stop off to see noteworthy buildings. I remember especially Fountains Abbey and when Maurice made a detour to show us Southwell Minster and the Chapter House with its exquisitely carved stone leaves. We were also taken round the great cathedral and its library at Durham. We often passed near castles but seldom had time to explore them. In Yorkshire I remember how thrilled I was when we were shown round the tiny Georgian Theatre Royal in Richmond which had only recently been re-discovered. The painted panels were rather scratched as it had been used as a warehouse for many years, but we could still see the designs. It was a strange sensation to stand on the stage and before the fireplace in the dressing room and to wonder if Sarah Siddons had played there. We hoped that, one day, we would act there ourselves, but this proved impossible.

I remember with pleasure our walks on days off, especially in the Langdale Valley, and near Redmire in Wensleydale, and along the cliffs at Cemaes bay where Johnny Ringham and I were 'harrassed' by a flock of about 200 sheep who insisted on following us as we crossed the field. We were soon completely surrounded by the menacing creatures. I expect they only wanted a turnip or two but we felt distinctly outnumbered and quite scared.

One Excursion Led to an Alarum

For some reason some of us had spent the night in London and Pam and I decided to go to an exhibition of paintings from Munich before meeting the others at Charing Cross Station to catch the train to Ashford in Kent. We mis-timed it (the traffic was worse than we had anticipated) and we reached the barrier to find the train steaming away and the others leaning out of the window waving frantically. We consoled ourselves that trains were fairly frequent and that there was plenty of time before the show. When we got to the school, the van had been unloaded and the company were preparing the stage. Maurice must have been very worried that we would not make it in time — he was livid, quite literally, and could hardly speak to us he was so angry. We tried to laugh it off, pointing out that there was still time to do our chores and that we hadn't been late for the show — but we had been very shaken. Maurice was tight-lipped for several days and I don't think either of us ever took such a risk again.

Epilogue

In the late 1970s I returned to The Warren. We were on a journey from Hay-on-Wye to Exeter and I found we could take a route through Aylburton. At first, I got us lost in the lanes but eventually I found the right way. There was a large sign saying 'Private' at the end of the drive, which was rather off-putting but I persuaded Rob to continue on towards the house. No tree spirits welcomed us (the car was lower than Bertha) and the old house looked somewhat forbidding. There was a new building by the farm. We parked at the bottom of the steps and I climbed up and tapped nervously at the door. A woman carrying a baby opened it. She looked at me rather suspiciously and I said, 'I hope you don't mind but I used to live here and, as we were passing, I just wanted to show my husband and daughter what the house looked like.' Her husband arrived and I told them about The Compass Players. This interested them as she had, at one time, wanted to be an actress. They had not lived there long and I think he was a chemist and was commuting from London via the M4 and the Severn Bridge. At last came the question I had been longing for: 'Would you like to look round?'

It was strange to be back, so much had changed. The hall and dining room had been completely panelled in a smooth light wood (I think taken from a German liner), and the cupboards and Holy Water stoup had disappeared. The bathrooms had been modernised and there were huge skylights in the attic roof. I told them as much as I could about how it used to be and what we did in each room. He asked me about the ornate gilded mirrors in the 'Rehearsal Room' and wondered if it had been a Music Room. I couldn't remember them at all and suggested an intermediate owner had put them there.

In some ways I was glad we had been but I missed the warm atmosphere and the continual bustle of the house as I remembered it. I don't think I shall want to go back.

Addenda

In one of my notebook diaries I have listed some of the things I had to do for the costumes for *Great Catherine* in 1950.

Soldiers
Black coats
turned back (2)
cuffs
pockets   Boots   shoes
collar   guards
buttons
epaulettes

Varinka
white tights
Lady's Dress — Dolly Varden hat

Patiomikin

    Lieutenant's coat let down
    gold braid
    new collar
    braid round arm

1950 notebook expenses include:

Beaucaire	1/3d.
(this appears frequently — by 1951 this was 1/6d.)	
Silko	4d.
Lunch	2/9d.
Mending tape and safety pins	2/-
Anadin	1/8d.
Cellosene	1/6d.
French chalk	5d.
Soap	6d.
Bus fares	3d.
Stick greasepaint	1/3d.
(by 1951 this had gone up to 1/6d.)	
Watch strap	4/4d.
Surgical spirit	2/-
Meths	3d.
Dress shields	4/6d.
(anti-perspirants weren't much used in those days.)	
2 Leichner Liners	1/8d.
Toothpaste	1/4d.
Books	3/6d.

4

THE YOUNG VISITORS WHO STAYED

Collin Hansen and Raymond Parkes

Collin Hansen was born in Westport New Zealand where, as a boy, he experienced serious fires, floods and earthquakes. He still says his most memorable experience in England was being with The Compass Players. After he left them, and a brief spell living in Sweden, he came back to work for the BBC for over 20 years. Raymond Parkes was born in New Zealand and gained seminal experience in the amateur theatre in his home town of Hamilton, from 1934 till he met Collin Hansen in 1948. He taught in Westport for a year and they left for England in 1949. After The Compass Players he returned to teaching in London, which he gave up after a stroke in 1971. He examined in GCE English Literature and Drama until 1988. Collin and Ray are now retired and living in Bath. While they were with Compass Players they undertook many tasks and Collin organised the backstage stage management procedures for Dr. Faustus *with brilliant precision.*

In 1948, in New Zealand, if you were interested in the theatre, you would most likely have heard of Compass, and Charles Brasch (the NZ poet) had written *The Quest* for them. Brasch was published by Denis Glover, of the Caxton Press — one of the great achievements of New Zealand's pre-war period — and Denis gave us John Crockett's address. We had been experimentally touring *The Mollusc* (by Hubert Henry Davies) to mining villages, where probably no plays had ever been performed, and we felt that, if we could share the experience of The Compass Players, we might be able to form a similar group at home. We set off for England, with very little money but much enthusiasm and a determination to meet them.

(Later, John told us he had sent to D. D. O'Connor, a NZ impresario, a proposal to tour New Zealand and establish a company there, but he had had no response. Presumably O'Connor had preferred to back the highly successful tours of plays produced by Ngaio Marsh for the Canterbury College Company. How NZ audiences would have reacted to Compass's

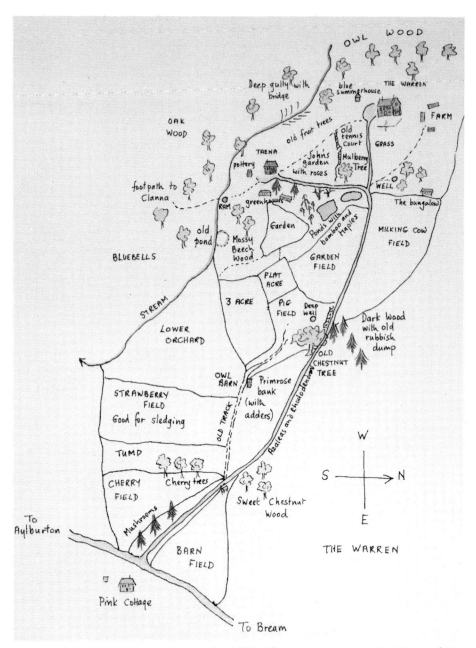

Map showing The Warren.   (*Ruth Ineson, 1989*)

The Warren.

Armine and Pam sewing, John gardening.

Lizzie and Anne, John, Collin, Johnny, Hedley, Maurice, Joyce, Pam, Armine, Martin. (Ray took the photo).

Rehearsal on the terrace.

The hall at The Warren. August, 1948.

The Warren, oil/canvas. John Crockett, c.1950.   *George. Pencil drawing.*

Taena and the Warren. Lydney, Glos. Scraperboard. John Crockett, c.1950.

Moura Deady and Hedley Lunn in J. M. Synge's Tinker's Wedding, *1948.
Photo by John Crockett.*

Mr. Fussy and his Clerks. Times Fool, *an English version of Holberg's* Den Studenlose *by John Crockett under the pseudonym 'Adam Angus'. First presented at the Library Theatre, Manchester, subsequently on tour, 1957. Masks by J.C. (Masks now in the Theatre Museum).*

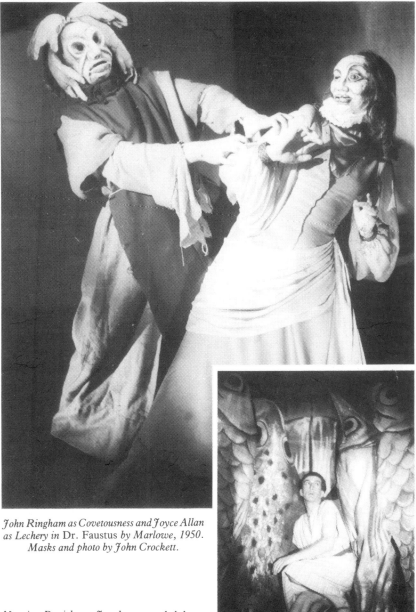

John Ringham as Covetousness and Joyce Allan as Lechery in Dr. Faustus *by Marlowe, 1950. Masks and photo by John Crockett.*

Maurice Daniels as Jonah surrounded by a goldfish, a red-herring, a plaice and a swordfish. Design and photo by John Crockett.

distinctive style we shall never know; but had that tour taken place our lives would have been very different.)

After letters, and a visit to meet John and Anne, we arrived at The Warren to spend the first week of 1950 when Joyce was being rehearsed. She had replaced Moira Deady, and *The Proposal* was also being run in.

From then on, Collin's brief diary entries reveal many of our immediate reactions:

'They indeed do precisely what we intend to do in NZ. They are more non-compromising than we — they consider Shaw positively low-brow, and will concede nothing to audiences.'

'The boiler was out of action and we slept in an attic at the very top of the huge house (what if there was a fire?), in extremely uncomfortable beds, but never mind.'

We were invited to join the company in Durham for a week later in January, as observers and helpers. The arrangement was that they would pay for meals, but we should pay our own hotel bill, and we went to Durham by train with gifts of rations, and loans of money from Auntie (Ray's aunt, without whose help we would have been forced to find some paid work). Our first date was at Neville's Cross (a large training college), with *The Last Enemy*. Collin noted the resemblance of this play to *Peer Gynt;* we immediately wanted to include it in our NZ repertory. In the evening there was a drama school, which the Players carried out from time to time:

'Then a long, immensely amusing and tremendously instructive series of scenes in which various things went wrong: over-acting, underplaying, lights that didn't work, bad prompting, bad movement, and finally, for a very good ending, bad curtain calls. Quite the most successful school imaginable.'

'It is all proving valuable experience...an extension of what we learned in *The Mollusc.*'

After Durham we had to find work in London — Ray appeared in a bad production of *The Provok'd Wife* at the Arts — and, shortly after we were settled in a flat, there arrived letters asking us to join the company in May, and we were 'to bring a large stuffed parrot'. (It was then fairly easy to buy such a thing, and we got one from a shop in Villiers Street for £3). When May came, we dropped everything, made our way to The Warren and began one of the most eventful and important years of our lives being, or trying to be, Compass Players.

....

Even though he was demonstrably a most kind person, there is no doubt we were in awe of John, but personal relationships with the rest of the company were remarkably easy. We were all from quite different backgrounds. Certainly John never lost a chance to have a go at Pam and

Armine because they had both been to drama school. Breakfast was a touchy time; we lot ate in the living room, John, Anne and Lizzie in the kitchen, where you went in and out with discretion, careful not to be chatty, bright, or to muck about. We, at the big table, buried ourselves in newspapers, books or scripts. Armine sometimes had a bit of a time of it from John. Her family were socially prominent and he never let her forget it. She was invited to a Buckingham Palace garden party (and we were all very impressed). John was furious and said there was no possibility of her being spared for rehearsals that day — he was most scornful of the whole business of garden parties, Buckingham Palace in particular. But for once Armine had her way and off she went. Afterwards she came straight back to The Warren, still wearing her big hat. We secretly, and with fascination, had her describe every detail. Probably each one of us had to put up with some similar experience, but it was 'poor Armine' (as we remember) who seemed to suffer most. After John had brilliantly designed the masks for the Seven Deadly Sins in *Dr Faustus*, he said one evening, 'I have moulded each mask on a personal characteristic of each of you who will wear them.' We thought a bit; then Armine said in a small voice, 'I am not all *that* envious.' What to say, what to do? She was not the sort to rush off in tears, but she would say honestly what we all felt.

We all agreed on political and social matters. In Durham Ray had bought a *Daily Telegraph* to read over breakfast and was rightly derided. (Auntie took it, and we had little knowledge of English newspapers then.) Those were the halcyon days of good popular newspapers, when the readers of the *News Chronicle* were treated as seriously as those of *The Guardian* and *Independent* now. They read *The Observer*, in order, as Anne not unseriously said, 'to know what to think'.

We were blissfully unaware of any emotional entanglements there might have been. Months later, when Joyce and Martin told us of their engagement, no one seemed surprised except us.

'When did all this happen?' Collin asked.

'In Keighley.'

'Keighley? But how did you find the time? That was the place where we stopped at the cafe at mid-day and there was a notice "Closed for Lunch". Surely that's all that happened at Keighley?'

But they found time, as lovers will.

John's dominance was such that we all submitted to it, it seems, without a murmur; it was the price you paid for his guidance. Shortly after we arrived at The Warren and still uncertain what to expect, there was an 'Annual General Meeting'. We were shocked at the financial state of the company, and wondered how they could possibly keep on going (and even more aware of their generosity in having taken us on in such circumstances). There was the perennial long discussion about how could we ever acquire the ultimate, a black velvet curtain-surround; the choice of a new play went on for hours ('No, not another potboiler' — *A Phoenix Too Frequent* was as far as they would go. Now Brand perhaps?). But all this was as nothing to John's final bombshell. While the company had been away he had redecorated the stairway; *someone* (an inevitability it seemed to us considering the traffic up and down those stairs) had left fingerprints. A lecture along the lines of, 'Would you do this sort of thing in your own home?' went on and on — it was well past two in the morning now. Everyone sat, guilty, and went to bed guilty, with finance, the new play and the black velvet surround submerged.

An aspect of life at The Warren was the absence of privacy and relaxation; we were all on the go from 8.30 a.m. or so till after midnight at the earliest. But one evening when there was to be a discussion with the Taena Community about Jonah, we could not face it and literally escaped to a pub on the road to Aylburton, buried (in our hazy recollection) deep in the forest. There we had a pleasant time drinking cider, looked at rather warily by the regulars. From their guarded questions and remarks we gathered that 'our lot' up there were at least free thinkers if not free lovers, and pretty weird. Next day, back at The Warren, our behaviour we felt, was not approved of but was not remarked upon despite the fact that we swore next morning that we had seen a UFO on the way home. Ray was more relaxed when Paula (Rice) and John Eyles spent a few days with us. They were very gentle, calming people, especially John, and their influence was welcome with so many creative people, some with strong personalities to cause clashes.

Life was anything but dull, and there were many happy moments. There was always something of a sense of drama at The Warren. The boiler played a continuous part in our lives; it was a wood stove, the only means of heating the water, and was so temperamental that no one could master it. 'I suppose you know about the boiler?' became a question all Compasses must remember with alarm. We still use it to introduce a disaster, or an unexpected success. Starting up the electric generator was a fearsome business, and we would have nothing to do with it, pleading hopeless ignorance of all kinds of machinery. It was said that upstairs was haunted (of course); sometimes Joss, the old, old dog, would stare up the stairs for an hour in an un-nerving way, rather like Thurber's dog, growling and bristling his sparse hairs. Once a hornet zoomed in on us during a peaceful evening and set the place in a panic, and during the week its nest had to be located and destroyed. Collin raised alarms about snakes, the first time when he found some slow-worms under a large stone. We undertook to dig the big vegetable garden which John had made and on which all depended, and one day Collin came rushing in again crying, 'Snakes!' John took some persuading, but this time, sure enough, it was an adder among the Brussel sprouts, and John killed it with a fork, looking magnificently like George and the Dragon. (John told us that once he had been sunbathing naked on a rock in Cornwall when he heard a faint rustling; turning his head he found, on either side of him, two adders sunbathing also. The story has become part of the Crockett legend, accounts of it varying only as to the exact number of snakes).

....

The rehearsal period lasted until the first perfomance of *Man Overboard* on 14 September in Malvern, and in retrospect was not much fun, nor, indeed, very instructive except perhaps negatively — learning what not to do. It was, though, never dreary or boring because there was always so much to do: making the masks for *Dr Faustus* (days and nights of pasting); preparing for the mimes with exercises run by Anne (which we kept up for several years and wish we still did); making bread for twenty people at one stage, and endless washing up; Collin doing the office work and trying despairingly to establish and impress on us a stage management routine for *Dr Faustus* — there was not a moment when someone did not have to do *something*, rehearsing two long plays, *Man Overboard, Dr Faustus* and the short, but complicated, *The Great Catherine*. We particularly recall the making of the huge curtains for *The Great Catherine:* they were of hessian, and John had cut big blocks of the Russian Eagle which had to be printed on it in red and black. 'Printing' them meant that the block was covered with ink, then laid on the hessian, then we in turn stood, stamped and jumped on it until the imprint was made. Several days of this and we could just about manage the stairs.

A silly quarrel with John had perhaps the greatest influence on attitudes that Collin took later. As he recalls:

'One morning John and I were having coffee and I was beginning to warm to him as the generous, gentle teacher that I felt he was. I asked, all unaware that only the ignorant fall into such pitfalls,

"Why do you not exhibit your paintings?"

"There is no need."

"But they don't exist until they are seen."

John's reply was long and academic and left me without a leg to stand on but I felt deeply (and still do) that I was somehow right. We got deeper and deeper into this complicated subject, John able to confound me with example after example, and I getting more and more stubborn until we both got bad tempered and the argument was never resolved. Looking back I think I let that quarrel colour all my subsequent feelings about Compass. The company existed (I decided) as no more than a means whereby John could project images he would have otherwise suppressed (yet it was impossible to imagine Compass without John); I began to find in all his writing and direction, in his use of actors and effects, the release of emotions he could not otherwise acknowledge. I got quite cranky about this: "He ignores

Marlowe's message and creates only his own *pictures;* in *Man Overboard* there is a line, 'You are all dead fish, wrapped in the worship of your master here', and I pounced on this: I brooded on something he said about 'people with an inferiority complex not untinged with a kind of persecution mania' — was he referring to me, or to himself?"'

Over the months we discussed this a lot between ourselves, unable (or afraid) to bring it out into open discussion where it just might have done some good. For, of course, why should John not have been entitled to think and behave as Collin imagined? We recalled his ambivalent attitude years later, after watching Dennis Potter's plays, and we asked was it unfair of him to unload upon his audience the pain of his agonising early years? Yes, we agreed it is justified when it makes good drama. John may have done that too, using his actors as he did his 'secretive' brushes and paints.

John's rigid direction worked marvellously with a play like *Comus.* If we thought he tended to suppress emotion in his actors, here that did not matter, where the indestructible verse could successfully compete with the beauty of the stylised movement that John created. It was so successful that we felt it unfair to suspect that John really preferred puppets and paintings to people.

Rehearsals for *Dr Faustus* were exciting; it was a most inventive production, with so much action; but we hated *Man Overboard* from its first reading. No one can dispute the dramatic content of the story of Jonah and the Whale, but the Old Testament has really said it all. In John's version it was painfully drawn out. It seemed to be the cause of all our woes throughout the whole time we were with Compass, and began with Ray's temperamental fit at the first run through. The lighting was complicated to say the least: the storm at sea; Jonah being swallowed; the scene inside the whale; and the last act, lasting 25 minutes, opened at sunrise and closed at dusk. John could not, or more likely would not, acknowledge that light cues need almost as much rehearsal as lines, and he shouted with impatience as Ray wrestled with our switchboard and tried to produce from it the effects he demanded (a modern lighting sysystem would have been stretched). After literally shaking and kicking the board Ray began to shout back that he had not the faintest idea where any light was, and a halt was called (it was about 2 a.m. now) for everyone to cool off. Months later on tour, Collin, too, had to be calmed down: crossing under the stage he knocked his head badly and Ray found him staggering about. 'What am I doing in this except helping John to have some sort of conversion? I look ridiculous, I feel ridiculous, I *am* ridiculous!' He was shushed up and, strangly, for the remaining performances before we left he felt contented in his small part, having perhaps learnt an aspect of an actor's lot, that it is not what you think of a play but what you can make of it. Making the most of it or not, we do not think anyone was very happy with *Man Overboard.*

Our switchboard was a fiendish affair and quite capable of short-circuiting the town supply despite Martin's wizardry in linking it up, no doubt often quite illegally. It had to, and did, achieve remarkable effects (John always got his way in the end) and these would sometimes call for three or even four of us to work the dimmers. It was, of course, portable, but only just and was horribly heavy. Carrying it up the long stairs at Lydney Town Hall, where Compass had their dress rehearsals, Collin felt a sickening lurch in his stomach; three years later, in Sweden, he had the operation for the hernia that had been triggered. Our lights, too, were large and cumbersome and difficult to place; one, known as 'Gertrude' was a vicious thing, capable of giving you a nasty kick. Touring companies today should bless the electricians for their modern equipment (though we sometimes wonder why they need *so much* of it).

The last days of rehearsals were hard going — we once worked until four in the morning, and were never in bed before two. We never thought it would be all right on the night; but, 'It will be all right, and quite different when we are on tour,' the experienced ones assured us.

....

And so it was. In spite of the relentless schedule we found everything less frenetic. Maurice, in a quiet and confident way, was in charge, and he and John Ringham shared the hazards (and dangers) of driving. The long journeys covered a huge area of England, Wales and southern Scotland, and we would sing, read, argue and discuss and try to ignore the cold and the weariness that always intruded. We particularly remember hilarious renderings of *Comus* in the accents of the places to be visited (it has quite a new dimension in a Yorkshire accent). The joys were often, for us two, our own particular delights: we were seeing a new country in the best imaginable way in the company of intelligent friends who educated us better than could any travel or guide book; we were meeting a whole range of people whose views and ways of life were different from what we had known. There were, too, the 'company' delights: days out when we had no performance date and we would have a picnic in the country, visit cathedrals and places of interest; wander (once we two climbed up much of Langdale Pike in quite inadequate footwear and clothing until warned by a sudden and menacing descent of cloud); and if in a dreary town we might actually 'go to the pictures', and for *free* what's more, on our Equity cards. We were always hungry, but there were Pam's 'company teas' in the dressing room; we would pool our coupons and Pam always managed to find delicious cakes and buns which were difficult to buy — she once got a pot of Marmite. These feasts were surrounded by costumes being ironed and cleaned and all the varied personal repairs that had to be made. Gerard (Martin's father) once made a memorable remark about dressing rooms (there was rarely more than one); he saw us only occasionally and was pleased with everything 'and no hanky panky in the dressing room'. 'No hanky panky' was used thereafter in all sorts of contexts, even to settle an argument when all else failed.

When in high spirits, we felt we 'were on our way' and that there was little more to ask for. We never asked ourselves if actors are made by touring; they learn tolerance, develop a feeling for people, learn to organise, how to see and analyse the countryside they are in, but to act? Is it not an art best nurtured and developed in better circumstances? Travelling on and on, mile after mile through rain and sleet, fighting weariness, the actor can have little passion left to show on the three boards where he may have to perform in Borgue.

Some of the hardships of touring are probably the same for small companies now. Things have become easier as living conditions have improved, but in our day there was comparatively little central heating and there were restrictions and shortages; it was not unusual to have to make do with a dressing room without running water, and there never seemed to be any hot water at all. None of us was obsessed with bathing, but we were often covered with a ghastly make-up mixture called 'wet brown', a sort of thick water paste which gave us an appropriate swarthy look. Slapping it on in icy winter was horrible and of course it had to be washed off before we could go to bed.

We realise now that we two had no true appreciation of what people had suffered in the terrible fuel and weather crisis of 1947; when John and Anne described the conditions they faced trying to tour that year, the reality was simply beyond our imagination. The winter of 1950-51 was nothing remotely like that, but sometimes Collin seemed to be so sorry for himself that now it is funny:

> 'We did *Village Wooing/Great Catherine* to a full house, the set teetering and not falling over by a miracle, and back-stage noises like a thunderstorm. Stayed with Mrs O. in a rather charming house: there are radiators everywhere, and it *appears* to be steam heated but of course they do not work, nor does the geyser in the bathroom, so again no bath. It is now seven days since I had one, and as the boiler is not working at The Warren I won't be able to have one there either. Even in the Western Desert I did not go so long without washing all over, and I think it not unlikely that the English never bath at all.'

> 'Next day: had a *cold* bath and was freezing all day. Loaded and arrived at The Warren about midnight and couldn't sleep for cold. Of course, the boiler is not working. Cannot think for sneezing.'

> 'We stayed at the tweeniest, tiniest place, very clean and sweet. In our bedroom pictures of "The Bridesmaid", "Alice", "Daisy and Fruit", "What is Home without a Mother", "Madonna and Christ", a Castle, a Poem and busts of George and Liz. No bathroom, of

110

course, and there is no hot water in the pub either. These two old dears somehow make do by charging only 7/6, and give an excellent afternoon tea for 1/-.'

'In very deep snow, in Derbyshire, we arrived at a B & B where, it was whispered around, there was a *bath*. There was, but it was newly arrived and unconnected, and the lavatory was outside. Next morning we had cold baked beans and a pork pie for breakfast before pushing and coaxing Bertha to leave the place.'

We found some peculiar places: a café where they did things in 20-minute bursts, 20 minutes to take our order, 20 minutes to bring all that was available, bread and butter, 20 minutes to bring some tea. They were not rushed because we were, not surprisingly, the only ones there.

Hospitality, the euphemism for staying with local supporters of the Arts group, was however nearly always restful and lavish. The mother and daughter of a Lancashire family came to the hall after we had packed the van, at nearly midnight, and collected us; as we drove up to the house the mother said, 'For God's sake take them and give them a drink,' — one of the most welcoming sentences we ever heard. She gave us a superb supper and we talked for hours. No matter how tired we were, we always enjoyed talking to our hosts, who were genuinely curious and interested in our lives and had lots of questions to ask. It must have seemed glamorous and adventurous to many; once a young man helping us with the slog of packing, asked, 'How do you get into this racket?' On another occasion we stayed in Yorkshire with a widow whose show cottage featured on the cover of *Country Life;* a sweet-scented cottage garden and a babbling stream outside our window. At Ampleforth College the fathers and brothers entertained us all after the performance, the senior pupils waiting on us with scrambled eggs, out-of-season fruit, and wine, and we became quite merry. The next morning the Headmaster, a terrifying, slightly hard-of-hearing giant, had breakfast with us, much pre-occupied, and there were wonderfully fatuous remarks by us all in attempts to engage him in conversation.

The halls and theatres we visited varied from a mere platform to the Library Theatre in Manchester. Sometimes there was no 'way round' from one side of the stage to the other unless you made a journey outside in the snow. Once this outside scramble had to be in the reading-room of the library; Maurice in his *Comus* costume — tights and a cloak and a fantastic body make-up — opening the window, climbing in and running through the room occupied by elderly and sleepy folk bent over their newspapers. We never did learn of their reactions. Audience reaction was always varied. In one area of Wales some of the audience whispered throughout *All for Truth,* and we learned afterwards that they were translating the rhymed couplets into Welsh for their non-English-speaking companions. Before our time — in Wales — some audiences almost involuntarily came down to the stage after performances of *The Quest,* so enthusiastic were they. Perhaps the most satisfactory reaction was that of an old miner in Durham who said of *Dr Faustus*, 'That's not high brow, that's *entertainment*,' perhaps the best comment on Theatre and a slap in the face to those people who still imply that entertainment has to be only light-hearted and to avoid fundamental issues.

A particularly memorable date was at Stamford Hall, the Co-operative College near Loughborough. It had been built by Sir Julian Kahn, in execrable, vastly expensive, 'modern' taste. (There was a pond on the estate built to house the seal that he gave his wife for her birthday, she presumably having everything else: later a second seal had to be acquired as a mate for the first). The superbly equipped theatre had been built solely to entertain his friends, and it had a remote-control, pre-setting switchboard and a 24-grid system. It was our first encounter with such a modern system, and we were ashamed that we could not make use of it, and were acutely aware of a serious gap in our knowledge. Some time later we made a return visit to perform *Man Overboard,* and this time Ray sent a light plot to their stage manager. When we arrived, this SM told Ray he would have to do it himself, as he had decided the play 'was blasphemous, and he was more concerned with his morals'. Reconciled that there was no accounting for the strange effects *Man Overboard* could have, Ray fiddled and practised all day with the technical marvel, but to no avail and we had to make do with some very odd and approximate lighting for the performance. Collin noted the two incidents with some gloom, as a warning of another issue that would have to be faced in the future.

By and large everyone stood up well to touring even though many difficulties never seemed to become easier. Performances would sometimes lose vigour because of exhaustion or because of the physical difficulty of getting them on to the inadequate stage. John would descend on us from time to time to tighten things up, which he would do thoroughly and we would feel better for it. All the same there would be tension for some days before. One awful visit was when he came on his motorbike; it was not a satisfactory motorbike, and he had to push it for the last few miles. He was at his most acerbic about the performance *(Dr Faustus):* 'The only good things about it are Maurice's performance and the masks.' We have, thank heaven, forgotten the next day, remembering only how willingly we pushed him off on his return journey.

On our penultimate date, in Amlwch, the company outnumbered the audience and we exercised our traditional right of not performing. This failure to attract did not surprise us, because we saw no posters in the town or any advertisement that we were there. We relied for advance publicity (and ticket sales) on the enthusiasm of the local Arts organisation to whom we sent posters, photos and so on. This naturally varied according to just how good at organising the local secretary might be; otherwise we relied only on a minimum fee of £20. Collin mentions several times his doubts about this system, but could not come up with a better solution that would not cost money. The joint persuasion of Gerard and Maurice in securing dates was very successful indeed, but that was as much as they could do.. In this, and in many such ways, perhaps Compass had indeed progressed as far as it could under its present organisation.

....

The tour ended in April. Some time during the Christmas break we had made the very difficult decision to leave. We felt we were ungrateful and disloyal, but weighed many things. It is a measure of how difficult it was that we broke the news to John by letter rather than at a company meeting. He replied:

'There is little that I can usefully comment on. I can only say that I could have wished that you could have *said* these things to me and to the other members of the company. And that we have had many company meetings and a thousand opportunities when you could have discussed your disagreements, whether on 'principles' or on anything else. One of the reasons which made us glad to have you with us was that we thought you would both be able to bring something positive to the company, even though it was different. The Compass Players is not something fixed and unalterable, and it surely ought to be up to the individual to make his contribution at all times; but as far as I know neither of you has ever raised your voice in discussion of any sort, nor, for that matter, declared what your principles are. This seems to me salient... I am sorry that you are unhappy but there seems little that we can do to help but to release you at the earliest possible moment. Finally, may I say how very sorry I am, and how disappointed.'

We had been cowardly in not doing as John said, but we did not have enough confidence in ourselves to do so, and retained too much the feeling that as 'new boys' we could not presume to influence or direct them in any way. We instinctively felt that the days of the small, independent touring company were numbered. Compass was being blindly optimistic if they really believed they could go on as they had begun and were still operating; eyes were closed against the reality of economic necessity. We dreamed about having the black velvet curtain-surround; but there was the greater need for many more absolute necessities — a new van, new lighting, different promotion. The company *had* to be restructured and compromises would have to be made, and we could not believe John would have ever tolerated such changes as these, and it was impossible to imagine his ever sacrificing an ideal or independence. Before long the company would have to find a permanent theatre, just as the similar Theatre Workshop found out. We doubted that their rigid opposition to Arts Council help was wise, but to have questioned that decision would have been heresy. This summing up is with hindsight. Even if we had been able to put it to them at the time we now think that perhaps Maurice might have been the only one to analyse it coolly; John would surely have brought down the fires of Hell, the others would have been uneasy and distrustful of this shifting of the earth beneath their feet. But, again with *hindsight*, we should have dared.

Without support, we alone did not feel able to raise such questions, and to have insinuated, to have tried to win them over one by one, to have 'plotted' behind John's back, was unthinkable. We deplore the ridiculous top heavy organisations of many companies now, where sometimes there are more administrators than actors; Compass were the reverse and seemed genuinely to believe it possible to keep going by ideals alone. Collin wrote: 'We are miserable with them most of the time, will always be outside them, and have lost faith in their work'... This was not really true, we felt miserable because we felt we were living in some sort of never-never world.

We lost touch with John and the Compasses. In the 1970s we saw Steven Rumbelow's production of *Faust* (The Triple Action Theatre). Rumbelow is a painter who came into the theatre in order, he says, 'to paint with people'. His work is in direct line from John Crockett. Did Rumbelow ever see a Compass production, we wondered? Perhaps as a small boy at school? We cannot know what influence Compass had on theatrical development, so much of what they began is now accepted, commonplace practice.

When we went to see the posthumous exhibition of John's paintings, we were deeply moved. Collin revised all those thoughts which had stemmed from that argument long ago; we decided that anyone lucky enough to be part of that process of artistic presentation should submit to it, for there is an undreamt of wealth to be learnt from it. We went to see three paintings in the Church of St Hugh of Lincoln at Radstock. One of them is the Resurrection of an aggressive, defiant Christ and the features are those of John. 'Typically John,' said Fr Dominic, the parish priest; he said it with a kindly chuckle that showed he knew him pretty well. The Radstock friend with us asked again about John: Collin told him: 'He was a director of The Compass Players. No, *he was The Compass Players.*'

We never did return to New Zealand. Collin went to the BBC and Ray returned to teaching, then to examining in English and Drama. We retired to an old mill in Somerset and made a garden there and then came to Bath. It is difficult to realise now that we were with Compass for less than 18 months; nearly 40 years later that period, the Players, John and his many faceted influences affect us as strongly as ever.

5

THE TRAVELLING, THE PLAYS, THE REHEARSALS

John Ringham

John Ringham has continued to be a professional actor throughout his life and hopes to practise his craft until he dies. He also writes: two books, nine plays for stage, (four of which have been produced) and a play for BBC radio. He lectures, most recently for the Anglo-German Friendship Society in Germany. He has a German wife, four children and a large allotment to feed them. He plays the piano daily, almost exclusively Bach, his passion for whom stems from Compass days.

I have had two strokes of major good luck in my life and they both came in the shape of people. I'd like to be able to claim that I recognised the luck when it dropped into my lap but I was too young, believing that such things happened to everybody in one way or another. I was simply being given my ration and I was content to ride it. Intuitively at least I knew I was on to a good thing, and that's something.

John Crockett was one of those people. The other was a woman called Jay Vernon. Jay came five years before John and without her I wouldn't have met him. Between them they have shaped my professional and private attitudes to everything I have done — and still do — and without their influence my life experience over the last forty-five years would have been less fulfilled and less exciting. How is it possible to repay that kind of debt?

Jay Vernon deserves more than a passing reference but her influence was on others who, with the single exception of myself, had no contact with The Compass Players. Brief details of that influence, however, are relevant to this narrative.

In Cheltenham, Jay ran The Falcon Players, an amateur group in Cheltenham for teenagers, throughout much of the war. The repertoire was invariably classical — Shakespeare, Greek drama *etc.* — and she expected and got hard work from us all. That would have been enough for most people, but not for Jay. The theatre wasn't only a place to go to for a bit of entertainment; it was a way of life requiring commitment and dedication from those who worked in it. It could open the doors of the mind to the unimaginable, it could help people to understand others, and that a great play like a great piece of music could show that man was capable of creating great good as well as great evil. And we, The Falcon Players, were privileged to be a small part of this great whole. This was heady stuff for teenagers whose ideals had yet to become tarnished.

With such high-minded aspirations the move from Jay Vernon to The Compass Players seemed natural and easy.

Like the majority of my generation I left home to do my national service in 1946. Even during that period I appeared more than once in Falcon productions when I came home on leave. By the time I was demobilised in 1948 the need to become a professional actor was overwhelming. And characteristically Jay did all she could to help and encourage. In the autumn of that year she showed me an advertisement in the *New Statesman*. It asked for an actor who could drive to join a fit-up company, and the contact was John Crockett whose wife, Anne, Jay had known a few years before.

Within a few days I was at The Warren auditioning for John. I stood in the rehearsal room and delivered Confession's speech from *Everyman* and the Messenger's speech from Euripedes' *Electra*. I was offered the job. At twenty I naturally assumed it was my self-evident talent which had made me successful. Wrong. Sometime later I learned the real reasons. Because of nerves my diction was poor and John had found it difficult to understand what I was actually delivering but the choice of audition pieces had impressed him. So did the list of plays I'd done with Jay. But what finally turned the balance was that I could drive. It was a relatively rare qualification in those days but an essential one for Compass because Maurice Daniels was carrying the full load of driving at the time, plus the job of company manager.

Neither of us had a full licence.

He had been driving for some years in what was then the Belgian Congo on an international licence which wasn't valid here, so he used a provisional one. I had taught myself to drive during the war and, since there were no driving tests then, I had taken out a full licence. But during my army service I'd let it lapse and tests had been re-introduced so I had to use a provisional licence too. However, as long as we drove with someone who had a full licence, all was quite legal, and Armine Sandford held one which, like me, she'd taken out during the war. I'm not at all sure whether she was able to drive at all but Maurice and I were covered. It was a bizarre situation, resolved when Maurice and I took our tests later in Worksop. By pure good luck for me, the examiner had been a major in my army unit in Egypt. I was treated to the full old pals act and was passed, I've no doubt, because of our previous association. Maurice, ludicrously, was failed. He was an excellent driver with ten years or more experience behind him. Perhaps the major felt he'd gone over the top a bit with me and thought he ought to balance things up. Maurice took another test later and passed easily.

It's likely, in retrospect, that I could drive little better than Armine. My only experience had been on motor bikes and my father's little Morris 8; I had certainly come nowhere near driving a large goods vehicle. But I was very young and totally confident that I could drive anything, and in the event I suppose the feeling was justified. I dare say the others had one or two bad moments when I first got behind the wheel, but a blithe ignorance carried me through potential disasters.

I joined Compass in the December of 1948. I felt comfortable, a round peg in a round hole, working in a job I loved full time instead of part-time.

The travelling

I was put in charge of Bertha. A van, no matter how skilful the engineering, is no more than an internal combustion engine fitted into a framework of wood and metal and placed on four wheels to get it from one place to another. Naming such things smacks of the sentimental. But Bertha was different.

Drivers of the old steam locomotives grew fond of their charges and indulged them in their idiosyncrasies. I developed a similar affection for Bertha and she deserved the name she had been given. She was a 1937 Bedford van with a long wheel base, registration number DML 800. (I normally never remember any other than my current car's number.) She was painted dark blue and on one side had been painted swathed curtains in red and yellow and 'The Compass Players' in white between them. 'The Compass Players' had also been painted on the front, but the other side of her was nothing more than a sweep of dark blue from end to end; no legend and no curtains.

She was already eleven years old and she was not in showroom condition. The speedometer no longer worked and, therefore, neither did the mileage indicator. There was no self-starter and she needed cranking to get her going. It was also necessary to keep a bottle of petrol handy to pour into the carburretor before she would start, but that was all she asked for. True, there was a knack in getting the starting handle in exactly the right position before turning over, but having established that degree of rapport she would fire and tick over contentedly.

'Bertha' is a name which suggests diligence, reliability and a sense of responsibility without, perhaps, much sense of imagination. Our Bertha was all of these things. We couldn't afford temperament. Sometimes - rarely - I would dream of a sleek new van with shiny chrome everywhere, bright new paintwork and a more powerfiul engine but never for long. It was almost like being unfaithful to her and she didn't deserve that sort of treatment.

She had a loading space about 12 foot long, 6 foot six high and 7 foot wide. Sometimes we were touring five productions which meant space was at a premium. The 7-foot hessian screens always travelled, so did the 12 dimmer switchboard and the 24 lamps — some of them 1000 watt lamps, which were bulkier than today's models —, and there were costume and prop skips, a backcloth, curtain-surround, collapsible rostra of various sizes and a great number of bits and pieces like screen braces, counter-weights, battens, electric cables, headers for the screens *etc*. The first load-up with new productions at The Warren would take the best part of a morning. It was a large three-dimensional jig-saw with no room for error, and, when the roll-door finally closed on everything, nothing more could be squeezed in. It was an impressive piece of work and often our hosts doubted that all the chaotic muddle lying around would be packed away. In fact it was no different from the sort of necessity fairgrounds, circuses and travelling players had faced for centuries. After two or three loading sessions we were able to finish a show, strike everything and pack and stow Bertha ready to move off in an hour and a half. Only the occasional date like Abergavenny, with a hundred steps to negotiate to the hall on the top floor, were the exception.

The front of Bertha had been adapted to carry the company. This was through the generosity of Pam Goodwin's father. Windows had been placed behind the driver's and front passenger's doors and two double bus seats fitted. In front there was a bench seat for two beside the driver. When seven of us were touring it was comfortable enough but when Collin Hansen and Ray Parkes joined us, bringing the numbers to nine, we prayed for short journeys. It was not luxurious.

In the four years I was with Compass we played all but three or four of the counties of England, all the counties of Wales, and the Lowland counties of Scotland. How many miles that represented I can't even guess at — the speedometer and the mileage indicator were never fixed — but it must have been massive, especially when you add the mileage the company toured from 1944 onwards. As far as possible dates were arranged so that we were not playing Devon one night with a school's matinee in Cumberland the next. We needed roughly four hours to set up and an 80-mile drive was the maximum we could readily manage in a morning. Bertha did well and the roads had to be good if she was to average between 25 and 30 mph. She was not a racing car. On a good day in a good mood she might manage 55mph but she was happier at 40mph. I suppose at a guess we must have travelled around 25,000 miles each year. It may be more; I doubt very much if it was less. Despite careful planning there was always a time when we needed a day or even two to drive from Anglesey to Kent, or from Northumberland to Pembrokeshire. While I was with Compass Bertha plodded through the lot, and that with only one change of engine.

One journey stands out as being unusually trying though I expect others in the company will remember some they would rather forget. It is a good example to take in many ways, summing up our and others' attitudes.

We were rehearsing new productions. In the middle of this period we had a series of dates booked in Stranraershire and Kirkcudbrightshire, lasting for about a fortnight. Our finances were near rock bottom. It was probably around this time that we acquired six fourteen-pound tins of peanut butter and a quantity of turnips. This was our staple diet while we rehearsed and I still can't face either of them.

The tour was to start in Drummore on the Mull of Galloway, 402 miles from The Warren and it had to be done in one trip because we didn't have enough money to afford a bed and breakfast stop on the way. I estimated it would take us about 24 hours including stops for food, so we planned to leave at around nine in the evening, drive through the night and arrive at Drummore in the evening of next day.

We were taking only two productions so we had a very light load. There was enough room in the back to set up a makeshift bed so that Maurice and I could get some rest between driving shifts.

None of us relished the thought of that journey.

We left The Warren in darkness and made for the A49. We drove through Hereford, Leominster, Ludlow and Shrewsbury and stopped at a transport café near Warrington around five in the morning for breakfast. There was a long queue in the café and it was packed. Our three girls were the only women in the place, apart from the girl serving behind the counter. We were all too tired to bother about whether we looked out of place or not, though it was obvious we weren't long distance lorry drivers. (Come to think of it, though, that would certainly seem to have been one of our jobs.) When eventually we reached the front of the queue the girl refused to serve us.

'Transport drivers first,' she said.

It would be childishly satisfying to record that one of us found a few choice words to say. Maurice, if anyone, may have done for all I know but I for one was feeling too demoralised to protest.

We crossed the border into Scotland in the early afternoon. We'd only driven a few miles when a police patrol car stopped us.

Two policemen got out and strolled towards us, looking without much enthusiasm at Bertha. They came to the driver's window. I was driving.

Did I know there was an L plate on the front of the van but none on the back?

No, I said, lying in my teeth. (We'd lost it a few days before and I hadn't replaced it.)

Could they see my licence?

I showed them my provisional one.

Who was the qualified driver?

I told them.

They looked incredulously at Armine.

Could they see her licence?

Armine found it and showed it to them.

One of the policemen drifted off to inspect Bertha. His colleague looked at us — grey-faced and tired — and an eyebrow lifted.

Where were we going?

I told him.

Where from?

I told him that too.

Let's see the log book.

I found it and showed it to him.

His companion returned. One of the back tyres will need replacing soon.

Yes, I know.

How much play is there on that steering wheel?

I showed him. There was rather a lot. (A few weeks later the steering gave up altogether when I was overtaking on a narrow road.)

That needs fixing.

Yes, right.

Sound the horn.

Ah. It doesn't work.

Who were we?

Actors.

Ah! Eyebrows rose higher. Let's see your travel log.

Our travel...? What is...? I didn't know we were supposed to have one.

We were a commercial vehicle, weren't we? All commercial vehicles should have a log of journeys.

Oh!

You don't have one?

No.

They looked at each other. Eyebrows threatened hairlines.

By this time, thank God, there were the beginnings of a smile on one pair of police lips. The one who wasn't smiling turned to me with disbelief that such things were possible in a modern world and then quite gently read me the riot act. Dumfries was a few miles ahead. There I would buy a journey log book, buy an L plate, check the steering, get a new tyre and fix the horn. We will be stopped again in the near future so get it done.

Yes. Fine. Right.

(We *weren't* stopped again.)

The police grinned at each other as they walked away, one of them even laughed as he got into the car, and I heaved a sigh of relief. It was a long list of misdemeanors.

Everyone was far too weary to rap my knuckles and I drove off putting as good a face on it all as I could. We arrived in Drummore late that evening. Maurice and I were very tired but the others were feeling ill. They'd sat for hour after hour with nothing to do, cramped and unable to sleep properly. It took the adrenalin from the performance the next evening for them all fully to recover.

I did stop in Dumfries as the police had said I should and did as I had been told to a great extent. I didn't get another tyre. There was still some life in the old one and we hadn't got the ready money anyway. Nor did I get the steering fixed. I should have done that. When it finally broke I was very lucky not to have a serious accident. It was, with one exception, the nearest we came to a smash, at least during my time with the company. I was told of an occasion before I joined when Anne Crockett was driving — at that time the company had a large and old single decker bus — and, as she was approaching a roundabout, she was given so much conflicting advice about which direction she should take she drove the bus straight across the grass of the roundabout itself. As a compromise that seems to me to be eminently practical, though I suppose not to be recommended for general practice.

My one exception was when we were returning to The Warren late at night and in the autumn. We had just left Gloucester on the road to Lydney when we ran into very thick fog. I reduced speed to little more than a crawl, but it wasn't slow enough. A lorry suddenly loomed ahead of us only feet away. I slammed on the brakes quickly enough to prevent us ploughing into the back of the lorry. What caused the damage was a large wooden joist jutting out some feet behind it. It smashed through our windscreen and, with me straining backwards in the driving seat, stopped inches from my face. The rest of the drive home was bitterly cold.

I cared for Bertha as well as I could within my given capabilities. If that sounds defensive it is because my capabilities were very limited mechanically as they still are. I kept her topped up with oil, used a grease gun reasonably regularly and in winter drained her radiator on any night when freezing temperatures threatened. This last may have been the reason we lost our one and only performance because of a breakdown, but I hope still that it wasn't my fault. The calamity which hit us happened after we'd been driving for two or more hours and I think we would have been in trouble well before if I hadn't done my job.

We were due to play a public school at Pocklington a few miles east of York one Sunday evening. The Saturday afternoon before, we were driving through Bradford expecting to arrive in Pocklington early evening. Right in the middle of Bradford great clouds of steam suddenly erupted from the radiator. I stopped, got out and opened the bonnet. The engine was hissing ominously but there was nothing obviously wrong and I had no idea where to begin looking for the trouble. One by one the company gathered round, more as a gesture of solidarity than intending to give advice they were unqualified to offer.

Then Armine said, 'What's that?'

She was pointing at a thin line on the engine block.

'Nothing,' I said with irritating male chauvinism, and to ram my superiority home began to fiddle dismissively with electric leads and the carburretor and anything else to hand. That was a mistake. Most things under the bonnet were very hot.

It was November, very damp and darkness was closing in. I was clearly left with no alternative but to go and look for a garage. I found one quite close by, explained my problem and returned with a mechanic who turned out to be the owner of the garage.

He looked under the bonnet, straightened after a few seconds and pointed to the thin line Armine had noticed. We had a cracked cylinder head. I knew this wasn't a good thing. The whole engine would have to be removed to replace the block. That was a time-consuming job and time we didn't have. Apart from the performance at Pocklington the following day we would have to be on the road again Monday morning.

There is no way to explain the kindness which followed. We must have appeared a strange group in that man's eyes. Seven people dressed in clothes which had seen a lot of wear, speaking standard actor's English which bracketed us in the middle class, and all travelling in a battered old van; altogether a curious combination.

Maurice and I explained why the situation was so serious for us; what we did, what we needed to do, where we needed to be and how desperate we were. If we didn't work we didn't get paid. What motivated that man to commit himself so totally I don't know but he told us he'd get us on the road again in 24 hours. Where he expected to find a suitable cylinder block at that hour on a Saturday I've no idea. But he and a colleague worked long into the night, all Sunday morning and well into the afternoon, and in the process performed a small miracle. Bertha was ready to be driven away at the time he had promised she would be. Maurice dealt with the bill. They seemed more than satisfied with what they had been given and our happy gratitude must have been very obvious.

Pocklington School showed kind understanding too. Maurice had phoned to explain what had happened to us and they said they'd look upon it as a postponement, fixed another possible date and wished us well.

Considering the demands made on her, Bertha had relatively few breakdowns. For nearly four years Maurice and I drove her in all conditions. Heavily laden, she took us through ice, snow, fog and rain with a dogged toughness which belied her age. The roads of post-war Britain were adequate for the amount of traffic they had to take, but only just. There were no motorways and there weren't many dual carriageways. And because we played small villages and isolated communities we often drove along narrow roads and country lanes, some of which weren't suitable for Bertha's size. But, whatever the conditions, Bertha was always responsive for she held the road well and steered tightly — despite the one lapse — and, provided you indulged her in double de-clutching, the gear box was smooth. And her engine pulled sturdily even when negotiating the 1 in 6 gradient of Honister Pass in the Lakes.

Those journeys, however, were often tedious, especially for the non-drivers who had nothing to do but sit. And if we were playing the

Lancashire cotton towns, or the Black Country, or the Welsh mining valleys, or industrial Yorkshire, the view was bleak, especially on wet days, though there were always compensations which came mostly from the welcome we were given in these places by so many of our hosts. And close by the scars were the Black Mountains behind the Valleys, the Vale of Evesham close by Walsall and Wolverhampton, the unspoilt length of Wensleydale as well as the view across Tremadoc Bay from Harlech, the Burns country of Dumfrieshire and Kirkcudbrightshire, the black-earth levels of Holland around Spalding, the Devonshire moors, the Pembrokeshire coast and Gower peninsula, the Peak District and the great spread of the Lakes. When we were within shouting distance we'd take time to see Ludlow castle, Stokesay's fortified manor house, Hadrian's Wall, Southwell Minster, Fountains Abbey and all the great collection of cathedrals.

The tradition of the travelling player is very old. It isn't difficult to imagine a troup of actors touring *Oedipus Rex* from Athens to Thebes and across to Corinth and Argos, riding in carts with their props piled around them, hoping to finish up in some decent digs in Adelphi, and doing it two thousand and more years ago. The mediaeval strollers, rogues and vagabonds, plying their trade from village to village, were our direct ancestors. Whether we chose to be or not, we too were detached for much of the time from society. Our contact with others was always fleeting. While they returned to their homes and families we piled into Bertha and drove off into the sunset. This romantic picture isn't altogether divorced from the reality.

We were a tiny unit, self-contained and in many ways self-sufficient. Our worldly possessions were minimal, in some cases packed in their entirety into hold-alls squeezed into the back of Bertha; our 'home' was The Warren which we saw for only a quarter of the year; we could arrive, unload, do a show, pack up and be gone, leaving only the memory of a show in a few people's minds to mark our passing; we had few creature comforts; we were long-distance lorry drivers, electricians, stage hands, costume and wig makers, furniture removers, managers, designers, writers, directors and, finally, actors. What we had, however, was a shared belief in what we were doing which made it easier for us to accept a life-style others might think of as foolish.

Be that as it may, travelling was fundamental to our purpose, a philosophy if you like. People make philosophies work and Bertha earned her place too among the people. It would hardly have been possible without her or something similar to her. Her design was practical rather than beautiful, she bore the scars of narrow gateways and she needed a coat of paint badly; but if it is possible to be anthropomorphic about a Bedford van, then she had many of the qualities needed to make Compass work. I remember her with affection.

123

The plays

Enter four horsemen, galloping.

Even Drury Lane Theatre with its huge stage would find that difficult to bring off. However, someone clearly thought that that sort of thing was run of the mill for Compass and sent us their play with that memorable phrase as its first stage direction. Moreover, their confidence in the limitless resources we were assumed to command was reinforced two pages later with another stage direction: Enter two opposing armies. Shortly afterwards they engaged in a battle; infantry, cavalry and cannonades.

Clearly, to stage that particular epic would call for imagination both on the part of the audience as well as the player and producer. Despite the fact that some of the stages we played were very small — Coleg Harlech's was a large semi-circular bay window —, and we would have had some difficulty in assembling the top brass let alone their battalions, it could conceivably have been staged by us. Dramatically there is no reason why two opposing armies should not be symbolised in the persons of two actors wielding banners and, using stylised movements or dance, fight out a battle. Nor is the problem of horsemen insurmountable. The Kirov Ballet have a famous sequence where Cossacks ride in tremendous style across the Steppes and there isn't a horse in sight. Nor are elaborate sets necessary. Elizabethan audiences were content enough to let the words paint in the set for them. The Chorus in *Henry V* is a case in point. But if the play is badly written you have loaded yourself with a quite unnecessary handicap. And that script submitted to Compass was very badly written.

Good productions with skilled actors can create near miracles with poor material. Certainly with technically accomplished actors it is possible to shape a scene which has no shape, build climaxes which don't exist on the page, play against lines to make a dramatic point, and with authority and superimposed conviction make characters interesting who would otherwise be dull. And when in doubt, shout. But why bother when you can do a well-written play? The actor's job has enough built-in problems without adding to them unnecessarily.

There is another, important factor to add to the argument. It is easier to act in good plays. A great play can be almost actor proof — if not producer proof. An indifferent performance of *King Lear* or *Antigone* can still leave an audience feeling that it has been in the presence of something powerful and greater than themselves. Why, then, pass over the advantages that gives? It will be clear already that Compass' policy was to present plays of some quality. Such drama, it was argued, is not the exclusive property of an esoteric few, enjoyable only to the cognoscenti. Provided fine plays were entertaining and presented entertainingly, they should be accessible to anyone, anywhere, with the price of a seat. The trick is finding the right play.

In the very early days of Compass, when the company consisted of four players the choice was limited. Small cast, full-length plays in those days were few and far between, let alone plays with real quality. Today in the 1980s one-man shows and two-handers have become much more commonplace, simply because to produce them costs less. Except for the large subsidised companies like the Royal Shakespeare Company and the National Theatre, few managements are prepared even to consider plays with casts of 15 or 20. But this is a financial not an artistic choice. Compass Players had to find plays which fitted their limited resources, limited that is in the number of players available. Doubling of parts was inevitable and this was a device used by the company throughout its existence. To do it successfully required ingenuity, imagination and a great deal of hard work, but those three qualities were always present from one source or another.

The alternative to a full-length play was a double bill — traditionally box-office poison but with Compass it seemed to work: Tchekov's *The Proposal* with Shaw's *The Man of Destiny;* John Madison Morton's *Box and Cox* coupled with Christopher Fry's *A Phoenix Too Frequent.*

The final option open to the company was to commission plays expressly for it. R. H. Ward's *Of Gods and Men* and John Crockett's dramatisation of Chaucer's *The Pardoner's Tale* are two excellent cases in point. The drawback here was always financial. The company never had enough cash in hand to tempt a writer and we had to rely on goodwill, which attracts only a very rare kind of person.

Even when the company grew in numbers, choosing a play remained a major problem. Company meetings taking place regularly turned just as regularly to discussions about finding plays. They were not comfortable meetings. Each member of the company had the right to put his viewpoint; nor was this an empty right. We were all expected to contribute.

It is now far too long ago to remember details of those endless meetings. They were anxious and troubled, that is certain. Yet out of them programmes evolved. Milton's *Comus* needing dance, singing, verse-speaking as well as acting — and difficult acting at that. Your sister is suffering a fate worse than death and an old shepherd decides the moment has come to reminisce at great length about many things before he feels the time has come to tell you where she might be. Tricky stuff when your brotherly inclination is to be off and at the villain. All this emerged from one of those meetings; and so did *Den Stundenlöse* by the 18th-century Danish playwright, Holberg. Somehow, somewhere, someone had come across a translation of this very funny play and it went into production and toured as *Time's Fool.* And the poetess, P.D.Cummins, a friend of the company, offered us her translation of Molière's *Le Misanthrope.* This was another popular play on the road, though I doubt very much if P.D.Cummins saw much financial return for her splendid effort. I hope she did rather better when John Crockett directed the play for the Icon Theatre Company at the Lyric Theatre, Hammersmith in 1962.

Of all the plays mounted by the company Marlowe's *Dr Faustus* was the most ambitious. The company was augmented to nine with the arrival of Ray Parkes and Collin Hansen, but there came a time when we were to perform this play with only eight people. Some of us had five or six parts to play. Even Maurice Daniels playing Mephistophelis doubled up as Pride in the Seven Deadly Sins sequence. In many ways it incorporated the qualities of a Compass style. There was a great deal of music, there was dance, mime, complex lighting and profligate use of imagination by John Crockett in its production. In performance it was a marathon, a non-stop feat of memory to be in the right place in the right costume saying the right lines in the right sequence.

The rehearsals

To make the first night of any production successful — and the actor's definition of a first-night success is to get from A to Z without disaster — adequate rehearsal is vital, particularly so in the case of a play like *Dr Faustus*. Compass normally allotted four weeks as a minimum rehearsal period.

Today, at the RSC and National Theatre, six weeks and more is not uncommon. Provincial theatres make do with much less and in the late 'forties three weeks was considered luxurious. For Compass Players four weeks was rarely enough time because it was never only a question of learning and playing a part or parts. Everything else — costumes, sets, props, stage-management — had to be made and organised at the same time.

Many actors as they get older, and I count myself among them, find the rehearsal period the most satisfying part of the job. I'm aware of the built-in absurdity of that statement since it is patently clear that the whole object of an actor's life is to get up in front of audiences and entertain them. And there does come a point, sometimes as late as a dress rehearsal, when the actor feels the need of an audience, especially in a comedy. He needs confirmation, say, of whether he has judged accurately where the laughs should come, and playing in front of an audience is the only way he can know when, for example, to sacrifice three small laughs in order to play for one big one. But that is a playing technique and quite different from the rehearsal technique.

Rehearsal is the time when the actor is at his most creative. There is a lot of high-flown talk about the 'creative' artist and the 'interpretative' artist but the distinction is very fine. The initial creative process has begun with the playwright and his contribution is, it goes without saying, vitally important. But it is a contribution, not an end in itself. He has written it, knowing it will pass into others' hands because it will only truly live when it is performed. If he had wished it to be otherwise the playwright would presumably have written a novel. The theatre is essentially a communal art

126

form which involves the talents of many people and, if they are to do their job properly, they must behave creatively.

There are those who argue that the actor's job is simply a question of learning some lines and saying them loudly and clearly. What then is the actor supposed to be doing when a playwright indicates there should be a pause? Does he become a statue for two, three or more seconds and then reanimate himself to say his next line? Or, to use a close analogy, do four string players tackle a Beethoven quartet simply by playing the notes accurately from the page? Surely in the process of interpreting Beethoven's intentions they create mood, form, balance in their own inimitable style. The listener can choose the particular performance he prefers but by then he is exercising his privilege of artistic taste. The entire process which has enabled him to do that has been a creative one by all concerned.

Actors' rehearsal time is a period of progressive excitement and conflicting emotions. Having read the play several times and understood the playwright's intention behind the play most actors come to the first reading with confidence that they can play their part in it. This confidence is often quickly undermined when the rest of the cast present their performances, because the inflections, pace, style and mood they use are not always as one had imagined they would be when reading the play alone. It is at this point that the good director — ideally the first among equals — begins to draw all the separate performances into a unified whole. The rest of the rehearsal time is one of exploration, discovery and creating a unity of purpose. It can be a very exciting process.

Much, however, depends on the director. Without exception in my experience a good director always stresses the importance of the text. John Crockett was such a one. The first week at the very least was spent sitting down reading the play again and again. This was a process John had learned from Maurice Browne who had directed plays for Compass before I joined. It has a great deal to recommend it.

As we read, John would frequently cut in sharply with, 'I don't believe you!', 'You think *what?*', 'Top him!','You're not *listening.*'. Of all his injunctions this last had the deepest influence on me subsequently. The ability to listen to what your fellow players are saying is a fundamental and obvious necessity. But it is very difficult to achieve. In rehearsals especially, but in performance too, the actor's mind is full of many things: are we playing this too slowly, am I in the right position, why did I say that line in that particular way, should I use that gesture, should I throw that line away, what, for God's sake, is my next line? But if you develop a habit of listening many of those problems disappear. Take as an example a simple line like, 'I won't be there tonight.' It doesn't need much imagination to see that it can be said in a very great number of ways which directly affect the way in which the answer, 'Very well', is said. If the actor doesn't listen, not just to the words but to the motivation behind them, there can be no truthful interplay

127

between them. If he *does* listen his instincts will guide him, and technical difficulties are reduced proportionately.

By the end of a week of reading, the play could have been performed as a radio production. The shape of a scene, an act, the play was beginning to be set; so were the changing moods, the style and character relationships. We had been able to concentrate through the words on these aspects of our performances. By the time we came to setting our moves we had firm foundations to help us; how our characters moved, walked, stood, came much more readily. And after a week of concentration on the words, the process of learning them was no longer difficult. Lines are learnt as a series of thought processes — one line sparks off the next — and that is what we had exclusively worked on. These factors produced a greater sense of freedom at a quite early stage in rehearsals, allowing us to move ourselves with a minimum of direction from John who only needed to interfere when masking took place or groupings looked uncomfortable or sightlines became fuzzy.

Apart from the length of rehearsal time there was another unusual feature of Compass' approach to work — unusual, that is, for the time — and that was a daily half hour or more of limbering up before rehearsals began. Today actors are expected to sing and dance simply because so many stage shows are musicals, and many by habit limber up physically and loosen up their voices before rehearsals or performances start. In the 'forties the line separating straight theatre and musicals was clear and few crossed it, but because so many of our productions needed mime if not actual dance, some regular training was vital.

Each day started with limbering up at 9.30 a.m. and continued for half an hour or so, but longer if there were dances and mimes to choreograph. We would rehearse through until 5.30 p.m. or 6 p.m., have supper and then start work on the stage-management side of the production; costume making, props, masks, new sets as well as maintenance and repairs on screens, rostra, lights, Bertha, and all the paraphenalia of touring. As the days passed we worked longer and longer into the night until we reached dress rehearsals, and the hours we were able to sleep shortened.

And apart from the rehearsals used for performance we needed technical rehearsals because we were our own stage-management. These needed very careful organisation. Each of us would have a list of what we were to do, and as we exited from a scene we would say out loud, 'I now go to the switchboard and change a light sequence,' or, 'I now put on Richard Strauss's *Ein Heldenleben* and then do a quick change', or, 'I now lower the tabs on Act I.' A fly on the wall would have been vastly amused at this behaviour, but, of course, it saved a great deal of time once we got to a dress run. What's more, chronic tiredness had already set in by this stage and the only way to get the routine into our heads was parrot fashion.

Dress rehearsals are now only a hazy memory. One session of them, however, remains indelibly on the mind and it is one which I hope never to experience again. Certainly in forty years I've never known anything quite like it though, in the days before Equity set a limit to working hours, directors in repertory theatres have been known to give notes for a couple of hours immediately after a dress rehearsal which has finished at one in the morning.

We had rehearsed two new productions at The Warren. They were complex technically with intricate lighting changes, several scene changes and a long list of music cues. *Man Overboard* — John Crockett's play about Jonah and the whale — was one of the productions and this involved an almighty storm at sea which subsequently in performance drew comments from members of the audience that it made them feel seasick. A courteous exaggeration no doubt, but John had directed the sequence with great flair. Britten's storm music from *Peter Grimes* was playing, lights flashed, actors reeled helplessly about the cluster of rostra representing the ship, and bits and pieces of the ship disappeared in the brief blackouts as she began to disintegrate, most notably when a cage containing a parrot vanished as a great wave washed over everything.

To make that sort of scene work it isn't enough to sit down for ten minutes with a cup of coffee and a cigarette and chat about it. It takes a lot of time — and we needed every minute available. It was decided to hire a hall in Lydney for a week rather than attempt to dress run in the rehearsal room at The Warren. But perhaps, before I go any further, I should explain briefly, to those who have no reason to know, what is involved when you get to this stage in rehearsal.

Hitherto everyone has been concerned mainly with acting their parts. There have been no costumes, lighting, sets (except token tables and chairs *etc.*) and the playing area has been marked out in chalk or tape. Once we moved into the Lydney hall, all the technical apparatus had to be set up first before any other work could begin. The set or sets are built and lights placed in postion. The lighting plot has then to be set. This is always a long process when the degree of light from each lamp is agreed on and changes of lighting plotted in the prompt copy. Each section of music, too, has its volume set and the exact phrase or note for its beginning written down on the plot sheet.

A technical rehearsal then takes place. This is a grinding, tedious process but a very important one. Actors are wearing costumes and make-up for the first time and the show is beginning to look something like what the audience will eventually see, but it is not a straight run-through. There is a constant stopping and starting again; going back over difficult passages where, say, lighting changes take place, resetting music volume when dialogue is spoken over it, furniture re-set if a voluminous costume prohibits free movement, actors adjusting their positions so that they are lit properly, solutions found to problems of costume and set changes, and so on and on. And on and on. Even with a separate stage-management such rehearsals always take many hours. In Compass the time was extended proportionately.

The next stage is what is called, accurately, a stagger-through, when a run of the piece without stopping is attempted. It is rare for these to go through without a hitch. In Compass it was virtually impossible. For the actor it is an unnerving time. His costume may still be giving him problems — they are seldom comfortable, particularly period costumes; he could be worried by a piece of business which was possible to rehearse only once the set was up; he could still be finding difficulty in finding his key light in a particular scene. For Compass there was the added stress of keeping in mind whether it is after this scene or the next that we go straight to the switchboard for a lighting change when we exit, or whether someone has remembered to leave the right record on the turntable because there won't be time to find it if it hasn't been done. While all this was going on, the actor was grateful if some of his mind could concentrate on the small matter of giving a performance as well.

After the stagger-through, the dress rehearsal proper would follow. By this stage it is hoped that everyone knows exactly what they are doing at all times and that a performance of the play can take place at a standard good enough for an audience. Well, sometimes you're lucky and sometimes you're not, but there is no need to dwell on that now. With a week to prepare two productions to performance pitch we knew before we started it wasn't going to be enough; not with normal working hours. And we were right.

The first morning we drove the five miles from The Warren to start work in the hall at around 9 a.m. By the time we'd finished that day's work everyone in Lydney was fast asleep. The working hours quickly lengthened and for the last five days we finished at four or five in the morning and were back again in that wretched hall by 9 a.m. We were tired before we began, because for the past six or seven weeks we'd been working late, rehearsing and making everything we needed. By the end of that week we were the walking dead. We opened somewhere with something. I remember nothing at all about it. It probably wasn't a disaster because I would remember that. I cannot believe, though, that we sparkled.

There are directors who think that mileage can be made from working everyone to a point of exhaustion for a first night on the grounds that given a creative rehearsal period instincts will take over and we will all ride on cloud nine above the purely technical skills of the craft. The intended result is exciting theatre. They may be right. Huge quantities of adrenalin pumping round the body can work wonders. Martin Harvey's wife, Nana, was known to have limped with two walking sticks into the wings because of arthritic hips and, on cue, thrown them aside and skipped onto the stage. Perhaps we skipped around the stage on that particular stage that night. I shall never know. But we certainly gave the Exhausted Thespian Theory a unique opportunity to work.

Most of this chapter, and much of this book, has demonstrated the ability of the company to work hard and for cruelly long hours. Perhaps subconsciously I feel a need to boast, to show what a sense of vocation and dedication can produce. I own consciously to a pride in having been a part of that company. Yet what in the end is there to boast about?

Talking on occasion to fellow actors about those years I have yet to see respect and envy shining out of their eyes. More often there is a gentle shaking of the head in a 'you needed your head examining' way. Discounting the implied criticism, they may well have a point. There were in-built dangers in that sort of set-up, both professionally and privately.

We led an almost monastic existence except in the area of celibacy. This last factor was to prove to be a major cause of the death of the company but something of the sort was inevitable. We were thrown together very closely and we were isolated. The tendency to think of ourselves as the One True Theatre was strong and there was a need to restrict an incipient contempt for those who did not measure up to our exacting standards of what real theatre ought to be. We were ignorant, anyway, of what else was going on in the British theatre. We had neither the time nor the opportunity to go and see other productions. Martin Heller and I usually used the brief holidays we had for an intensive course in West End theatre going. Once we managed six shows in three days. But three days out of 365 isn't a lot. It encouraged insularity.

Insularity is very bad for the actor. His batteries need recharging regularly with ordinary day to day living, otherwise the theatre will suck him dry and he'll have nothing left to give. All living experience comes in useful sooner or later. Our 'living experience' was limited to our small circle.

The relationships which developed in Compass were, I suspect, expressions of a need to loosen the restrictions the life-style placed on us all, an elbowing out of the walls which enclosed us. And the cold shower effect of long and physically demanding work on the sexual urges of a group of fit young people was very limited, particularly since we never met anyone outside the company for more than a few hours and you would have had to be a particularly likely lad or lass to have made hay while that brief sun shone. There was no choice but to turn inward on ourselves.

There was one other professional handicap we suffered and it is an important one. Throughout its life Compass was involved directly with a very small group of people, perhaps 20 at most over the years. Acting, like many jobs, is a constant process of learning. Working with other actors, and with as many as possible, broadens experience, especially if they are older actors. The theatre is an ephemeral art form and tradition is handed down by word of mouth. A great deal can be learnt from older actors even it is only on the negative level of learning what *not* to do. On the positive side what can be learnt from them is invaluable. We were all very young in experience in Compass.

Given that list of disadvantages, what was it that compensated for all those weeks, months and years on 15/- a week all found? Perhaps the answer or answers are already clear between the lines of this book but they are still worth spelling out. I hope, and to a great extent believe, they are shared by everyone else involved.

First of all, there is the effect on the individual as a person. We all feel a need to belong and if possible to be valued too. Each one of us in that company could feel a total interdependence, and I hope it isn't just rose-tinted memory which makes me claim we valued each other. We assumed automatically that each was pulling his or her own weight to the best of their ability. This developed a loyalty which was really quite outstanding. To this day I value that quality above all others.

We shared a deep belief in the value of what we were doing. Little matter that the big world outside didn't have The Compass Players constantly on its lips. Despite nationwide touring, only a few hundred in each venue will have been aware of our existence. But that in no way takes away from whatever achievements there were. If one person in ten thousand saw *Dr Faustus* and believed that his life was richer for it we were justified in what we were doing. That shared conviction strengthened the bond between us, and we felt a deep sense of fulfilment because of it.

The private and the professional became one, of course. It could not be otherwise for they are indivisible. And what I learnt from those plays and rehearsals has remained with me all my life. There *is* a greater satisfaction to be gained from appearing in good plays and there *is* no greater pleasure than working closely with a fellow actor, taking and giving. Because we all cared first about the play there was no question of egoism indulging itself. We wanted and needed to play together and not as isolated vacuums dotted about the stage. However unpolished the end result may have been, this quality of ensemble playing was our strength. And John Crockett, during those long hours in the rehearsal room, insisted on the play coming first, last and always; the individual had to be subordinate to the whole. I still believe he is right.

It would be wrong to put this forward as the ultimate truth or to claim that we had a monopoly on that truth. There have been occasions when it has been a pleasure, even a privilege, to play a supporting role with an actor who has a special magic, a star quality, and whose talent explores areas my own talent is incapable of reaching.

I have come to believe that acting is an exercise in applied technique which needs to be touched by magic. What that magic is and how it is achieved I can't explain. To allow it to *emerge*, however, I do know it is necessary to work and work and work on a part and the play so that all technical problems have been solved, allowing the actor to work fluently. A concert pianist does not have to think which note follows which in a swift scale sequence or where the climax of a phrase or movement occurs when he performs. His technique and preparatory work will have taken care of that. Just so with the actor. The elusive magic has now the conditions in which it is possible for it to emerge. But it doesn't always arrive, and when it does have the appropriate conditions in a particular production it isn't always there for every performance. And there is a difference of degree. We lesser actors are not blessed in depth as the great actor is. And yet the greatest of actors when asked to define the magic is incapable of doing so. It is reported that on one occasion Laurence Olivier gave a performance of such stupendous proportions everyone present, cast and audience, were aware that they had experienced something of unique stature. But at the end of the performance Olivier stormed off in a fury, followed by one of the cast who knew him well. Why was he so angry, surely he knew that he had achieved something exceptional? Yes, said Olivier, but he didn't know *why*. The spirit of magic to a unique degree had been with him that night. And to be a part of the process of helping to create that kind of elusive greatness, no matter how insignificant one's own role may be in that process, has its own measure of fulfilment. But such talents are rare. For the average jobbing professional actor such as myself there is a special pleasure in ensemble playing, giving and taking, to achieve a performance of a play which will uplift an audience. I know that the collective magic of lesser talents can be as potent as individual genius.

Acting, despite tribulations — or even perhaps because of them — is a joy. Even after forty years, I still find the process fascinating and exciting for its own sake. I have never for a moment questioned whether I was right in my choice of a job. I therefore think of myself as a lucky, even privileged man. In alliance with Jay Vernon's early training, I have absolutely no doubt that it is John Crockett and The Compass Players who are largely responsible for that gift. My gratitude will remain with me until I die.

....

There is a necessary coda to this narrative.

A few years ago I was filming for the B.B.C. on the Gower coast and when I had finished I decided to drive back via Cheltenham and visit my family. As I drove along the west side of the Severn early the next morning I was thinking of the work I had just finished, not really registering the small towns and villages I was driving through when, with a start, I saw the sign 'Aylburton' and the beginning of the village. I was within two or three miles of The Warren. An impulse made me turn off the main road, drive through Aylburton Common, along the narrow lane and then turn right up the hill which led to The Warren's drive. I stopped the car on the hill and got out to look across at the house. The morning mist hadn't lifted yet and it was totally invisible. I left it at that. The symbolism of the mist seemed appropriate enough. It was the past, now shrouded in its own mystery. I stood for a moment, remembering in the broadest of terms, the happy and for me important years I had spent in and associated with that house, but it was long since over. I turned, went to the car and drove off. Let it all lie in peace.

John died two years later and I went to the funeral. He was buried in Prinknash Abbey across the river from The Warren and there were many of 'us' there. The wake was held in Taena Community close by and there was a startling number of faces from the Community I recognised but hadn't seen for 35 years. John's brother Tony was there. He, too, I hadn't seen since Compass days. I looked around me more carefully and saw a growing number of people I associated only with The Compass Players. I found myself disturbed by the sheer quantity of vivid memories which flashed across my mind, so vivid I remembered details in staggering clarity. I had half-forgotten what an enormous impression those years had made on me.

So it was, then, that with Pam taking over John's proposal and organising the writing of this book I had no doubt when she asked me to contribute that I would be able to remember without difficulty relevant details and episodes. And so it has proved. The incident with Bertha and the Scottish police is a case in point. It is, I am quite sure, accurate. And if this was true for me, of course, it would be true for the other players. And if a creation like The Compass Players can make such an impact on a widely differing group of intelligent people, then its story is worth recording for anyone who may be interested.

That John will dominate this book I have no doubt — and in my view so he should — just as he dominated the ethos of The Compass Players. But he was accompanied in his quest by interesting and dedicated people of conviction who in most cases were prepared to put up with his sometimes outrageous idiosyncracies and frequent bad temper because all of us recognised that at the core was a quite remarkably talented man who was also capable of compassion and love and warmth. But also because all of us knew that The Compass Players itself was in its humble way greater than the individuals who worked together under John's leadership.

6

THE WARREN AND OTHER MATTERS

Joyce Allan

I asked Joyce Allen to write about living at The Warren as she spent more time there than the rest of us while she was waiting for her first baby. She took voluntary redundancy from Moray House College of Education, Edinburgh, in 1982 and since then has visited Denmark, Germany and Greece as part of an international team working with mentally and physically handicapped young people. She has been a member of the Children's Panel in Scotland for 13 years and serves on numerous committees where 'trying to keep their papers in logical order is a near full time job'. She lives near Edinburgh with her husband Martin Heller. They have six children and, at the time of writing, five grandchildren. Joyce still finds time to do occasional work for television.

My first contact with The Compass Players came about through a meeting with the actor Wilfred Harrison, who was at that time fund-raising for a brand-new theatre to be built in the Midlands but to be used to tour small theatreless venues across the country.

I had recently finished my course at the College of Drama in Edinburgh and was eager to get as much theatre experience as I could. The previous summer had been spent on what might nowadays be called 'work experience'. Two or three of the final year students had been drafted in to be A.S.M.'s on a Festival production called *Ane Satire of the Three Estates* by Sir Robert Lindsay of the Mount. It was to be staged in, of all unlikely places, the Assembly Hall of the General Assembly of the Church of Scotland and to be directed by Tyrone Guthrie. Now that was a tempting prospect. After all, the name Guthrie had cropped up in book after book on theatre during my studies, so that the opportunity to be part of this project was particularly exciting.

The play was unknown to theatregoers having been written in old Scots in 1540, but the version to be performed was the work of Robert Kemp, whose writing was well known in Scotland; Cedric Thorpe-Davie had composed some brilliant music for it. The cast was gathered from a well-established group of Scots actors as well as some young ones such as Stanley Baxter, straight from the Citizens Theatre, Glasgow, who played the King's Herald. The whole adventure was a mystery for the population of the 'Festival city'. Occasionally I would meet friends when I was out prop hunting during the rehearsal period, and, although they were curious, it was impossible to convey the production that was evolving. All those involved seemed aware that history was being made and that we were all a small part of it. We were all thrilled by the audience response which was in great measure due to Guthrie's vision and confidence in the adaptation and in the fine cast he had assembled.

After *Three Estates* anything else was going to seem dull by comparison, but when the next Festival came round I was pleased to be offered the chance to go over to the Abbey in Dunfermline to be ASM on a production of *The Saxon Saint*. This piece had been written by Robert Kemp, who adapted *Three Estates* the previous year. Rachel Kempson was to play St Margaret, patron saint of Scotland, and in the cast too was a young English actor, previously mentioned, Wilf Harrison.

Wilfred was at that time raising funds for Century Theatre, an entirely new concept in theatre, with a stage, auditorium and dressing rooms all on pantechnicons and capable of being set up in virtually any venue. It was easy to lure him into conversation about this project on the train from Edinburgh to Dunfermline. John Headley, the engineer/designer, was confident that it would work and Wilf was enthusiastic about seeing it completed within a reasonable time-scale. In the course of our conversations Wilf spoke about the Adelphi Players and Compass Players as being forerunners of Century Theatre. He mentioned the fact that John Crockett, who was the Director of The Compass Players was shortly going to have to replace one of his company and he suggested that I might contact him in case he might see me. It seemed an opportunity not to be missed so I wrote to John Crockett and went off to ASM at the Gateway Theatre in Edinburgh, which was owned by the Church of Scotland.

Eventually the summons came from John. He would be auditioning in London and would be pleased to see me. The audition was to be held in Lansdowne Terrace, in a lovely terraced flat in a Georgian square. The door was opened by an elderly gentleman with a crop of wiry white hair, wearing what looked like a hand-me-down safari jacket from Field Marshal Slim. He introduced himself as the company's manager and told me his name was Gerard Heller.

I was ushered into the drawing room which was lined with books and had a kitten sleeping in a basket by the fire. (I later discovered it was a toy, one of Gerard's eccentricities.) John was brisk, welcoming and gave me a distinct impression of urgency in the situation. My audition pieces were well prepared; they probably gave John little idea of my potential and the amount of effort needed to get a performance from me, but he must have realised that I was willing and strong. Being strong was an essential ingredient in being a Compass Player; how else was the van to be loaded?

Could I come to The Warren to begin rehearsals and be ready to go out on tour in the shortest possible time? This was November/December, so there was no time to hesitate about my answer. Yes, of course. My father thought I was mad, my mother thought Gloucestershire was the other end of the world, my other relatives raised their eyebrows to heaven and marked it down as another of my more hare-brained schemes.

The train for Birmingham went from the Caledonian L.M.S. station in Edinburgh, and I have to admit that by the time I got to Lydney, Gloucestershire, I knew my mother was right, it *was* the other end of the world. Never mind, I was there and now at least there was one person to meet me I had met before. But this was 'John the worker' and there was little time for pleasantries. Anne, his wife, was different; a warm glow came from her and made me feel that she was genuinely pleased I had arrived. We rolled up the drive to the house, avoiding the odd pothole whenever possible, but it never was a smooth drive. The Warren made me gasp. I had lived in a bungalow in Kirkcaldy, Fife, and latterly in digs in Edinburgh but this handsome house in the depths of the Gloucestershire countryside was straight from the pages of the history books and it was impossible to think of living there.

The Warren was not a vast mansion; it was a home, having started life many hundreds of years previously as a chapel connected to Tintern Abbey, so there were arched windows, the floor was of flagstones and there were niches for religious statues and what were probably holy water stoups in the main room. Presumably it had been a chapel in those days; for us it was our place to relax. I put my luggage into a fairly spartan bedroom upstairs at the back of the house looking on to the side of the hill, no view from there, but then I was the junior member of the company. I looked for my hot water bottle as it promised to be my saving comfort. The shades of the former hostel The Warren had been before the company was formed were still there, but then it was only to be home for short periods of rehearsals. When I went downstairs it was to meet the rest of the company: Armine, Pam, Johnny, Hedley, Maurice and Martin.

They were a really nice group, open and friendly and very, very busy. Obviously nobody wasted time around there since time was so limited. I had a hard job distinguishing the two younger men, but, once Martin explained that Gerard in London was his father, it began to fall into place and The Warren was beginning to cast its spell over me. Lizzie and Lally, the Crockett children, were to become an important part of my life but at that moment only Lizzie existed, slightly precocious, with a mop of dark brown curls and an unusually easy manner for a toddler in the company of so many adults. Lally (Alison) arrived 20 January 1950 but I cannot remember where we were at the time, somewhere in Co.Durham probably.

Rehearsals were really hard, so many things had to be learned fast and the patience of the others could only stretch so far. In what seemed like no time everyone was beginning to pack up and talk about loading Bertha. By this time I was well acquainted with Bertha and was almost able to appreciate the personality of the old lady but until the initiation ceremony of 'the load', masterminded by Maurice and Hedley, I had not even started to become an accepted part of the company. The rehearsal wing of the house was at the furthest point from Bertha's parking place and a steep flight of steps added to the difficulty of getting props, scenery and costume skips to the van. Everything had to be carried up and down those steps. Is it only the passing of time that makes me think we did not seem to mind too much? Perhaps because we took incredible care in loading Bertha, and there was a real pride in a job well done, once it was over.

Departures seemed to be always during the day, but when we came back after a tour it seemed inevitably to be late at night after the last show of the tour when we came bumping up the drive and swinging on to the terrace at some unearthly hour. At those times that flight of steps was unbearably steep and all we could do was drag ourselves up them and into the house and to bed, leaving the unloading for the morning. The Crockett family would be in bed and so we might creep into the kitchen to fight for the warmth of the Aga, disturbing Joss the dog and the cats in the process. Armine would have to fill her hot water bottle and I seem to recall making cocoa for the men. Everything came in catering size packets and it shocks me now how much we took the food supplies for granted. Later I came to appreciate how much organisation that side of the work called for.

Spring came to The Warren, and when we were there at that time it seemed like heaven to my northern soul accustomed to the chill winds of the east of Scotland. In front of the house was a terrace, a lovely place to sit out and gaze across the Severn Valley. Three or four flagstone steps led on to the 'lawn' of fairly rugged grass which served as drying space for nappies and sheets, a playground for Lizzie and a collapsing space for actors exhausted by rehearsals, and prop and costume making. It was a really useful spot within earshot of the rehearsal room, yet out of earshot of John when you wanted to let off steam and say what you really wanted to! John specialised in the short fuse. Poor John, we must have been a sore trial to him a lot of the time.

In the summer months at The Warren it never seemed to rain. The skies were clear blue and we rehearsed and lay around on the grass between rehearsals. Not once can I remember rain, only the heady perfume of the wisteria and the luxury of the warm earth when one lay down on the grass.

By the time the next winter arrived, Martin and I were married, and in July our daughter, Judy, arrived, after I had had a secret skipping session with the children's rope which I found lying down the drive among the azaleas. John bundled me into the sidecar of his motor bike and Martin, looking shell-shocked by the whole situation, climbed on to the pillion and off we set for the hospital in Lydney. Winter had done the state of the drive no good at all and the baby did not appreciate it either.

The Warren without the company there was a very different place, and my time during these months had been spent with Anne and John, getting to know them and the children. Lally, in particular, felt that little bit special because I had been there from the time of her birth, it was almost as if we became Compass Players at the same time. Rain was an inevitable part of those months and the banisters seemed never to be free of the garlands of steaming nappies waiting to be dealt with. Whenever it was possible I would head for the kitchen. Cooking was much more attractive than washing. I had inherited my mother's inventiveness in cooking and positively enjoyed creating dishes that Anne would look at and say, 'What is it?' Most of the time it worked. John was a vegetarian and the great chunks of cheese which arrived in the grocery box were a challenge it was hard to resist. Rationing was still in force and John would complain bitterly that 'his' cheese seemed to disappear faster than anything else. Anne would spend a lot of time bottling fruit in the slow oven of the Aga. The result was an enviable supply of fruit which we could use in the winter months when the company had to be fed. Freezers did not exist.

Because things were still in short supply and some unexpected bargains had come into The Warren at some time, there was always a lot of peanut butter in the store. It was packed in very big tins, and ideas for using it, apart from spreading on bread, were non-existent, that is, until my mother came to stay and discovered it. She had no idea what peanut butter was, but created some tomato soup that proved a great success, thanks to the peanut butter.

An unusual liking I developed during the months at The Warren was ironing; big flat irons specifically designed for an Aga cooker made it almost exciting, learning the trick of always having a hot iron when it was needed became a challenge... simple pleasures. Anne would read every evening and John was apt to draw a quick sketch on any scrap of paper that came to hand if something he saw interested him. He sketched Anne a great deal. She had a wonderful stillness when she was concentrating that must have made her an ideal sitter. Now and again he would catch the likeness of a baby, sound asleep, in her arms or mine.

Occasionally visitors would come to stay, parents when the company was there and friends of John and Anne from time to time. One day we had some guests who were to be very carefully cosseted. Promises of sponsorship and much needed funding hung in the air and Anne and I went to town with the O'Cedar polish. It was a warm day in early summer and we made the rehearsal room look like a French chateau with the help of some cunningly placed cushions and bowls filled with flowers. The meal was ready and I had gone to a lot of trouble to make the nearest thing I could get to an apfelstrudel to follow the vegetarian casserole. The pastry was next to transparent, it looked and smelled terrific.

The guests arrived, small chat began the proceedings and John led them into the rehearsal room to have an aperitif. The lady, who bore a strong resemblance to Mama Cass... remember her?... sat down in the wicker armchair and down and down until she was glaring up at us from the floor. We tried to make light of the episode but things were beginning to look black. John decided that lunch would put things back on course, so into the dining room we went. 'Mama Cass' announced that she could not stand nuts and hoped there would not be any in the food; Anne and I looked hard at each other, and said not a word. We had used my mother's trick with the peanut butter for the soup, the vegetarian dish was laden with cheese and nuts. As for the apfelstrudel, it would not have tasted half so good without the almonds. Nothing more was said, but we did not get the money.

Our neighbours were the old friends of John and Anne from years back who worked the farm and potted in the studio. They had formed a community called Taena and it was good to have them available. Connie Ineson had an enviable down to earth quality about her and it was good to have Connie there when questions arose about the troubles of being a new Mum. The months before the company split up and we returned to Scotland were so traumatic that I became drawn to the tranquillity which existed at Taena and was no longer to be found at The Warren. Anne was quickly coming to the point of committing herself to becoming a Catholic and joining the community in their commitment to the Order of St Benedict. The utter simplicity of the white-washed chapel they had created and the beauty of the office they said each day and the Mass were powerful forces and I was equally happy to be swept along at that time. In the cold light of day it meant facing up to the consequence of such a commitment. I felt I had no choice but to take instruction, once we returned to Scotland, and enter the church, even though it was creating frightening difficulties in our young marriage. The power of The Warren and Taena came into play (perhaps those monks from Tintern had a hand in it too) and Martin and I were received into the church together in 1953.

Thirty-five years later I still look back to those momentous times and wonder at how dreamlike it all seems in retrospect. What remains clear in my memory are, of course, the little things.

The kitchen garden, overgrown but truly wonderful as a place to escape to. Never before had I seen fresh figs growing and the sight of the pink flesh inside the first one I cut open remains vividly in my mind.

The big kitchen table, heaped high with the cornucopia of groceries once a week and the social visit that went with every tradesman's call. After all, it was quite a trek to the house, worth a chat at least and a cup of tea. What music there was in those voices of the Forest of Dean, Mr Jones the grocer especially.

Once I climbed the hill behind the house and went on until I saw Tintern Abbey ruins in the distance. At that time I had no strongly developed sense of history, but there was a little shiver down my spine mainly because I loved poetry and there it was, coming to life.

Leaving The Warren was really leaving 'home', and the bonding which has existed between the company members over the long years is firmly bound up in our memories and experiences of that old house. When in the death throes of the company, another base was being sought, it seemed possible to transfer people and props, but it would never have worked. The Warren was part of the magic.

....

Editor's Note

In the early summer of 1989 I was visiting friends in Mid-Wales and we travelled into the Forest of Dean in search of The Warren. I called at a cottage near St. Briavels to ask the way from a woman who was standing at an upstairs window. She phoned someone for advice and then reported back, 'He says its where they used to have the nudist colony.' She then gave me accurate directions. I was amazed that even now, nearly half a century later, the local people still maintained that the community was a nudist colony... and so the myths are made and stay with us.

When we got to The Warren the present owners, the Dismorrs, were very kind and showed us round. Although it was far more gracious than when I had last seen it, the gnarled wisteria still flowered over the door and the house exuded its old charm and wisdom. The visit was a happy experience and it was lovely to be so warmly welcomed.

That summer too I found Ruth Ineson. We had known her as the eldest of the Taena children. Now she had recently given up teaching at Birkbeck College to sheep farm half-way up a Welsh mountain on a hillside strangely golden with the flowers of laburnum trees. Ruth recalled some of the problems of being a child in a community, particularly in having to relate to so many adults. Most children have only two parents but in the community it seems that parental responsibilities were often shared. But as a place for children The Warren and the farm had been magical and she can still remember it in detail including the deep well and the traditional names of all the fields. So Ruth, a child of The Warren, has drawn us a map so that they may be recorded for the future. (see page 98).

On our first visit to Coleg Harlech we were surprised to learn that a German actor had signed up for the week. His name was Sigmund Giesecke and he was a member of the civic theatre company at Bochum on the Rhine, and he had come to Harlech as part of a holiday in Britain. Once we had got over our nervousness at having him in the classes at all, an experienced fellow professional sitting there expecting us to teach him something, he proved to be a great asset as his sense of fun and enormous energy transmitted itself to the others. He had fought on the Eastern Front and had been a prisoner of both the Russians and the Americans and his experiences had made him an avowed pacifist. He became a firm friend of all of us and paid us many visits over the years. He went on to work at many other theatres in Germany, appeared at the Edinburgh Festival, and ended up at the Schauspielhaus in Vienna where, sadly, he died of cancer.

....

By 1949/50 Compass Players' work had expanded a great deal and the administration and tours management had become an enormous burden for both Maurice and John — particularly for Maurice who did all the booking of the tours as well as playing leading parts in most of the productions. About this time my father had retired and he was asked if he would like to take on the job of arranging the tours. He was delighted to do it. He had once done a similar job for the Hirsch Quartet, and after a life spent in insurance he was only too pleased to be connected with an arts organisation again, however small. His flat became a stopping-off place on journeys through London, and a very useful place where John could hold auditions for the company. It was here that Joyce Allan, all the way from Scotland, came for her interview, was taken on, arrived at The Warren, and in less than a year was marrying me from that same flat, at Holy Trinity, Brompton. It was very much a Compass wedding with Johnny Ringham as best man and the company almost out-numbering the relations! After a very short New Year honeymoon at Cemaes Bay in Anglesey it was back to The Warren to rehearse for the spring tour. I think we were doing *Man Overboard*, John's entertaining version of the story of Jonah and the Whale. Joyce had to play, among other things, a plaice trapped in the whale's belly. She was encased in a fish costume, and because the top of the plaice was painted on the back of the costume, she had to do the whole part facing upstage, almost blind, and asphyxiated with the heat. A fine start to married life!

Living at The Warren was a bit like living at a boarding school — spartan conditions, hard work and a slave-driving headmaster, who inspired great respect and affection but whom we could have wished far away often enough! At one time the situation was aggravated by the fact that it was also a Youth Hostel, of which John and Anne were wardens, and we had to cope not only with being on top of each other but on top of an ever-changing stream of strangers as well. Thankfully this did not last for long; as the demands of the company increased John and Anne decided to give up the hostel. In addition to us and the hostellers there were also some ducks and two cats, a big black thick-coated half-Persian Tom called Tripod because he only had three legs, and a little grey Persian lady cat called Pussy. The story of these two and of how Tripod came to be the way he was makes a touching animal story. Tripod went missing for several days at a time when Pussy had a litter of kittens. She began, one day, to carry these out of the house and down through the garden. Several times she was captured and brought back, but she kept on trying again and again to escape until eventually she was left alone and followed. She went across the fields and into a wood at least a mile away, and there was Tripod, with a front leg caught in a trap, and the kittens by him. Pussy had been feeding him and her family, and had kept him alive.

....

It is said that all good things must come to an end, but it is sad that so often the inevitable end is made worse by bitterness and acrimony. Compass Players was no exception to this, and when the financial problems suffered by nearly all theatre companies, large and small, are mixed in with internal emotional entanglements, inexperience and personality clashes, and when the people most concerned are far apart so that meetings are difficult to arrange and much discussion, argument and decisions have to be undertaken by letter, then everything becomes much worse. In our case it was also very sudden, and as far as most of the acting company were concerned, unexpected.

John Crockett decided that he no longer wished to be Artistic Director and resigned. He and Anne were in the midst of a difficult time and he was determined that their marriage must be saved. He was quite right, of course, but the effect on the rest of us was unfortunate to say the least, taking away as it did the strong leadership which had maintained the company since its inception. I was elected to succeed him, largely I am sure because no-one else was willing to take it on, and also because I had no idea what I was doing!

In October 1951 Sheila Louden, our hard-working, under-paid and enthusiastic company secretary in London, was struggling to achieve charitable status for the company, having interviews with high panjandrums in the Inland Revenue Department (who, it must be said, seemed helpful and friendly) and having some success in straightening out our relations with the Tax Man so that the company could have a chance, at least to keep its head above water. Sheila wrote:

...I have an appointment at 11 a.m. tomorrow with Mr Woodford. Apparently he is a *very* important person, and I don't think he particularly wants to see me — so say a prayer for me, all of you, that it will go off alright. I am shockingly badly documented as the C. & E. file appears to be still at Lydney and I can't find a copy of our present Articles of Association, though I will have another hunt for these this evening. I have explained this to whoever it was I spoke to and asked them if they would have their copy available if it is needed and also the file of correspondence. I will do my best to get *exemption* for November. I think that, even if they won't give us another exemption, they may accept another deposit.

I am extremely flattered at being official Secretary — please God I don't end up in jail!...

My congratulations on being Administrative and Artistic Director — it sounds wonderful.'

She wrote again on 20 October:

'Mr Woodford and the other man who was also present, some sort of exemption expert, were exceedingly nice. I spent a solid hour with them...

Mr Woodford went on to say that as I had taken on the Secretaryship I had better know the facts about exemption. Apparently it is far more complicated than we had imagined, in fact he said that in some cases the Department themselves were doubtful and had to submit the case to their experts who specialised in exemption problems. We shall never again have such complete *carte blanche* exemption as we had before as they apparently have Inspectors who check their decisions and they have been rapped on the knuckles several times for being too lenient and too sweeping in the exemptions they have granted in the past. For instance, all schools are not automatically exempt as we had thought, even when they sell no tickets. State-owned or state-aided schools coming under the Education Authorities are all right, but privately-owned schools such as Public Schools, where they put a charge in the school fees to cover entertainments, are supposed to pay tax as they are counted as making a charge to the public — and there are various other cases — the whole thing simply bristles with difficulties. I looked so appalled when he was telling me this that he laughed and said I was not to worry too much as it wasn't as bad as it sounded and he didn't want to frighten us out of business.'

New Articles of Association and a formal Board of Management were needed.

The Board of Management was to consist of, among others, John

Crockett himself, John Headley, an actor with the Adelphi Guild Theatre, which was an associate company with us in The Guild of Independent Theatres, and R.H. Ward, the playwright. He was a fine writer and a very clever man, but someone that I, a rather young 23-year-old, found cold and rather intimidating. Richard became Chairman of the Board, or at least their main spokesman, and my personal difficulty with him did not make the next few months any easier.

While Sheila was sorting out the Inland Revenue, my father, as well as planning the spring tour, was writing begging letters to various notables in an attempt to raise the money to buy a new van as poor Bertha was in her death throes and no amount of string or elastic bands could sustain her for much longer. Added to this, a new home for the company had to be found, as the owner of The Warren, an old friend of the Crocketts, was also in financial difficulties and needed to sell it. I remember looking at a property in Bletchworth, but cannot imagine how I thought it could be financed! The company was on tour and, although we were conscious of problems, no-one guessed at the thunder cloud that was gathering to burst over us so soon. Six months later The Compass Players was dead.

John had also given notice that he wished to withdraw the guarantee of £300 which he gave to the bank to cover the company's overdraft. This proved impossible to replace and when it was finally withdrawn in February 1952 the fate of the company was signed and sealed. After 36 years I find it impossible to be sure of the proper sequence of events — or even of many of the events themselves. A mental automatic censor has shut off many of the more embarrassing moments, and the small amount of correspondence that I still have, mostly from Sheila and my father, tells me a lot about mundane matters of printing and delivery of programmes and posters, and a great deal about their ideas and valiant, generous and self-sacrificing attempts to help to save us. But the awfulness of the final company meeting in Hexham on 9 February — the date gleaned from an old tour schedule — and of the meeting with the Board at The Warren is only an emotional memory. Facts are quite blotted out.

In retrospect, why was it all so important? After all, at the end not more than a dozen or so people were involved. Did we struggle to keep going to maintain a principle — some ideals about taking theatre to the people — or was it only an attempt to save our jobs and what in its own weird way had become something of a way of life? I think it was both. Certainly I, and others perhaps, were living in cloud cuckoo land when we tried to convince ourselves that with no resources to back us up we would be able to raise enough cash support to take on the responsibility for a new home and a new van! Ten or twenty years later it might well have been possible, when public funding for the arts increased as it did rapidly in the '60s and '70s. As far as I know Compass Players never had Arts Council or other public funding, although our performances were bought in by many public authorities.

Nowadays the Arts Council supports many companies that have followed in Compass' footsteps and perhaps we fell, unluckily, between the age of the self-supporting Barnstormers and the modern high-quality subsidised Fringe Theatre and Theatre-in-Education. As regards the ideals, indeed, I did believe in them and still do. When I joined Compass in 1948 it was just a first job and do not imagine I had any other aim than that of working in the magical world of theatre and joining the ranks of my idols of the day. But in a very short while I had absorbed many theories about the importance of taking the theatre to remote and theatreless areas and of bringing live performances to young people in schools — ideas which, under the guise of words like 'spread' and 'accessibility', are embodied in the charter of the Arts Council itself. When I found myself, 25 years on, a member of the Scottish Arts Council, I strongly argued the case for small-scale touring and I hope I had some influence in promoting the work of 7-84, Wildcat, Winged Horse and other companies that do this work north of the Border. With three friends I even formed such a company, Prime Productions, and successfully toured a production of Ena Lamont Stewart's trilogy *Will You Still Need Me?* in 1986. In the days of blanket television coverage and satellite broadcasting it may be argued that to finance such tours is a waste of scarce resources and that everything should be poured into centres of excellence. I believe this would be very wrong. Nothing *can* substitute for the live performance, it never has done and it never will, and it is perfectly possible to be excellent on the small as well as on the grand scale.

I have no doubt that much of this came from John whose influence for good or ill (mostly good) has affected my whole life. My training and development as an actor are more his work than my immature and ineffectual efforts at drama school and I shall always be grateful to him for that.

Another even more profound influence and change in my life came about because I happened to join The Compass Players. It had nothing to do with acting, but a great deal to do with living at The Warren and with the friends and colleagues who lived there too. During the war, John had been a pacifist, and with some others had farmed in Cornwall. Calling themselves the Taena Community, this same group now worked the farm on The Warren estate. While we were there, after much heart searching, and having invited many representatives of various religious and philosophical beliefs to come and talk to them, they became converts to Catholicism. The Community became Oblates of Prinknash Abbey and had their own chapel in the farmhouse where they said the Benedictine Office. This whole story is told in George Ineson's book about Taena called *Community Journey*. Joyce attended many of the discussions and lectures before the final decision was taken, and continued to join in the services once the chapel was opened. We now had a daughter, Judy, and so Joyce could no longer come out on tour, and after a time she too decided that she wanted to become a Catholic.

The resulting conflict was the nearest our marriage ever came to breaking up. After Compass Players was disbanded and I was working at the Byre Theatre in St Andrews, I went for advice to the White Fathers who had a house in the town. I met Fr Riddell who gave me some books to read, hoping I would grow to understand Joyce's beliefs even if I could not share them. No pressure was put on me, but the more I read the more I found myself drawn towards the Church. Eventually we were both received in Edinburgh in 1953.

So the legacy that Compass Players has left to me has been three things: a life-long attitude to acting and the theatre, many long-lasting and very good friends, and Catholicism. Quite a bundle!

The final irony belongs to Bertha. On the last day of our last tour we were stopped by the police in Bolton. They condemned her as unroadworthy and ordered that once we reached The Warren she should be taken off the road. Poor Bertha. But her spirit lives on in many another hard-pressed vehicle as latter-day Compasses travel the country seeking to bring the treasures of World Theatre to as many people as can be persuaded to watch them. Good luck to them all.

....

Editor's note

In March 1952 the company broke up and started to follow their individual careers. John and Anne Crockett went with Taena to Whitley Court near Prinknash Abbey. John painted, ran drama summer schools and directed Peer Gynt *for the opening of Scunthorpe Civic Theatre. In 1959 he directed James Brabazon's play,* People of Nowhere, *for World Refugee year at St Thomas's, Regent Street. This led to the formation of the Ikon Theatre Company at the Lyric Theatre Hammersmith in the early 1960's. Then John joined B.B.C. television as a freelance director where, amongst other productions he directed for the early Dr Who series. But he found it difficult to fit in with the London media scene and accepted an invitation to join the staff of Downside School. There, for the first time since Compass days, he was once again able to combine his many talents in the service of the arts and education.*

He and Anne retired to his beloved Cornwall where he continued to paint. He died peacefully, after an illness, at Newlyn in October 1986.

EPILOGUE

It is only as time has passed that most members of The Compass Players have gradually realised the importance of the Taena Community during those years and the quality of life and support that the small group of people who formed the community gave to us during the long rehearsal periods at The Warren. A sense of a still spiritual centre. It is for this reason that I have asked George Ineson to write his description of his friendship with the Crocketts and provide us with an epilogue to our book. George is the founder of Taena, an architect, philosopher and teacher. He still lives at Taena in Gloucestershire and is a practitioner of the art of T'ai Chi. He writes about the Compass Players and the Taena Community:

It was the winter of 1940. I was standing outside a small Cornish cottage on the moors between Penzance and St Ives talking to Gerald Vaughan when we saw five young people moving their belongings into another cottage just below us. We thought up an excuse to call on them and this was one of those strange simple happenings which form the shape of the rest of your life. John and Anne, Anne's sister Bettina, and two friends of theirs became close friends with the community of six which we had started in the September of that year. We met often to talk and listen to records and John introduced me to much I had not yet encountered — and especially to the writings of Carl Jung. John's many-sided interests and abilities, his intuitive reaction to hypocrisy, his warmth and his anger — all this and much more led to a friendship between John and Anne and Connie and myself. John and Anne rented a studio in St Ives and were planning to set up an Arts Centre, but in the summer of 1941, they decided to join the community, making a precarious living with goats and a few cows.

By then we were working five smallholdings, with a family cottage on each and we began to feel that the separateness would begin to prevent us reaching any real mutual understanding. So, in the spring of 1942 we gave our notices to terminate the tenancies on three of the holdings, the families in the remaining two holdings deciding to carry on separately. We began to look for a larger farm, but wartime conditions made this difficult and six weeks before we had to leave we still had nowhere to go. At the last moment a small community near Ross-on-Wye offered us hospitality while we continued our search. In September 1942, John, Anne and Bettina, Connie and myself with our two children, a cat, a dog and two goats, left by train to Ross-on-Wye and a very unknown future.

After several months our money ran out and we agreed to disperse. Bettina left to work on a farm in Devonshire, John joined the Adelphi Players, Anne left to teach in a school in Lancashire, and Connie and I stayed on to continue the search for a farm and to work for a local farmer. Connie and I visited over fifty farms, mostly in wild out-of-the-way places and by the summer I was beginning to feel that we were not going to make it.

We had decided to give up the search when the estate agent rang me up about a farm for sale in the Forest of Dean. It was surrounded by woodland on three sides with a view sloping to the South with the River Severn about four miles away and the Cotswold Hills beyond. This was The Warren, a secluded mysterious place which was to become our home for nine years. Gerald agreed to buy it and give us a tenancy and we moved in during September, 1943. Over that summer Connie and I had moved to a small community which had just started a few miles away. Some of their members had then decided to join a large community called The Society of Brothers and the remaining family moved with us to The Warren. This presented us with a difficult problem — John and Anne were still intending to join us but the difference in views between them and the new family was considerable. Connie and I were somewhere in the middle. The questions revolved round whether we worked towards a specifically Christian basis or whether we carried on as we had begun, leaving each person to find their personal inner path.

We lived in the large cottage and wood bungalow and a new family moved into the large house to run it as a Youth Hostel. By the Christmas of that year three members of the community left us and Connie and I were on our own in the cottage. John and Anne arranged to rejoin us as soon as they could manage it and it felt as if we had begun again on a basis of mutual friendship and common interests. But the difficulty of integrating in face of the inevitable conflict still remained and we tried to run away from it, hiding behind a plan or theory which is only, in fact, a mask for the conflicts in our own hearts. In the summer of 1944, barriers began to appear between John and myself and I felt unable to face the resulting conflict. We were both being driven by forces stronger than ourselves which we only dimly understood; John by his vocation as a painter and I by this strange compulsion to discover 'community'.

But we had no means of holding together until we could learn to see more clearly, and the conflict rapidly divided the community into two halves. I think also that the difficulties were accentuated by the fact that neither of us had a strong liking for farmwork as such, and John and Anne began to plan the formation of a small group of travelling players as a creative way out of what had become an impossible situation. The Compass Players, started in the autumn of 1944, and in the course of time they built up a reputation for the sincerity of their acting and the high standard of the plays they produced, leading a life of hard work and little money to avoid compromising with the standards of the commercial theatre.

After John and Anne left us, other people joined and there were seven of us living in the cottage and the bungalow, with the two people running the big house as a Youth Hostel. John visited us and the apparently insurmountable barrier was bridged, we were again able to communicate. I suppose I always knew it must be so even in the most difficult periods of our friendship; we seemed to be related below the level of conscious choice and emotional conflict. John wrote: 'I believe the anchorite and the wanderer can be united, because in many ways they are not separate.'

We then met Toni Sussman, a Jungian therapist who had escaped from Germany just before the war, and her influence was to be a decisive one. She introduced us to meditation, to the East generally and to other works of Carl Jung. Several of us travelled to London regularly to see her and we began daily meditation periods at home. The outer political search had begun to turn inwards and the life of the new struggling Compass Players wandering about the country seemed a long way off. But the two people running the big house as a Youth Hostel decided to leave and John and Anne visited us to discuss the possibilities of The Compass Players taking over the big house as a rehearsal centre and permanent home. This took place in 1946 and the strange relationship between the opposites of The Compass Players and the Taena Community became an important element in the lives of both groups. Every three or four months the company would take up residence, and strange declamations would reach us while we were milking the cows, ending with the excitement of the week before the first performance. At this time Tom and Hazel with their two children became the wardens of the big house for The Compass Players and they soon became involved in the community and eventually joined us.

Woven into all this were the periodic experiences of a new Compass Players' production. These had a magical quality difficult to describe — partly due to knowing everyone concerned, partly to the unusual approach to acting, and partly because of the kind of plays they chose to perform. One production which I remember very vividly was *The Quest*, a dance drama written by John and his New Zealand friend Charles Brasch and danced to the *Fantastic Symphony* by Berlioz.

For several years the community was deeply involved in its inner search while The Compass Players were travelling the country, yet in a way this seemed like two aspects of the same search. The real difficulty came when, one by one, the members of the community were received into the Roman Catholic Church. From John's point of view, this was an apostasy — the Catholic Church being the home of authoritarian dictatorship and right wing establishment. He told me that this step would inevitably finish our friendship — fortunately this did not happen but there were times when we felt very separated.

Ronald and Hilary joined us in 1948 and it began to feel that, however slowly and imperceptibly, something was growing. We had started periods of meditation and the Divine Office and converted the old stables into a chapel. We had built up relationships with Father Bede Griffiths at Farnborough Abbey and Prinknash Abbey and, when the last of us were received into the Church, mass began to be celebrated every week in our chapel.

In the summer of 1951, The Compass Players were facing an internal crisis and holding a series of meetings. Gerald wrote to us about the farm — he would have to sell it during the next year. We started to look for somewhere else to live and to work out what was involved in being a specifically Christian community.

By the January of the following year The Compass Players had run into further debt and decided to close at Easter. The company dispersed to unknown futures. John and Anne, who were both under instruction at Prinknash Abbey, asked if they could both come with us if and when we moved. In February we had found Whitley Court, a farm of 130 acres adjoining Prinknash Abbey, but the auction sale was in four weeks time and we had no money. A totally unexpected cheque arrived by post, which enabled us to buy it, and we moved in during May.

The eight years life of The Compass Players had not only been a significant outer event. They and Taena Community had together lived through a complete inner cycle which was going to influence the rest of their lives.

Taena 1988.

APPENDIX A

PLAYS AND AUTHORS   **COMPANY MEMBERS**

* Indicates new play, adaptation or compilation. A season usually started in the autumn

1944 - 1945

Plays and Authors	Company Members
Abraham and Isaac — Laurence Housman	John Crockett
How He Lied To Her Husband — G. B. Shaw	Leslie Hardie
*Ernshaw — Wilfred Gibson	Zita Jenner
Village Wooing — G. B. Shaw	Paula Rice
The Bear — Anton Tchekov	Anne Stern
*The Secret Life — R. H. Ward	Producers:
	Maurice Browne
	John Crockett
	R. H. Ward

1945 - 1946

Plays and Authors	Company Members
The Fall of Man — XV Cent. Mystery Plays	John Crockett
The Strolling Clerk etc. — Hans Sachs	Maurice Daniels
*The Quest — Charles Brasch	Leslie Hardie
The Three Maries — Cornish Miracle Play	Wilfred Harrison
Malvolio Mock'd — Shakespeare	Christina Megroz
*The Cockleshell — Wilfred Walter	Paul Oliver
	Paula Rice
	Brian Stapleton
	Anne Stern
	Elizabeth Wright
	Producers:
	Richard Scott
	R. H. Ward
	Dances:
	Paula Rice
	Anne Stern

1946 - 1947

Plays and Authors	Company Members
*The Jester — The Story of the Fool in the Theatre Devised by the Company	John Crockett
Springtime of Others — Jean Jacques Bernard	Maurice Daniels
*Of Gods and Men — R. H. Ward	Hedley Drabble
	Paula Rice
	Anne Stern
	Producer:
	R. H. Ward
	Dances:
	Paula Rice
	Anne Stern

The Last Enemy — John Crockett
Adapted from Chaucer
Box and Cox — John Maddison Morton
Man of Destiny — G. B. Shaw

John Crockett
Maurice Daniels
Moira Deady
Eric Gadd
Dorothy Grumbar
Martin Heller
Hedley Lunn
Paula Rice
Anne Stern
Producers:
John Crockett
R. H. Ward
Dances:
Anne Stern
Paula Rice

Dr Knock — Jules Romains
Village Wooing — G. B. Shaw
The Tinkers Wedding — J. M. Synge
A Phoenix Too Frequent — Christopher Fry
(*The Last Enemy, The Man of Destiny,*
Box and Cox in Repertoire)

John Crockett
Maurice Daniels
Moira Deady
Pamela Goodwin
Martin Heller
Hedley Lunn
John Ringham
Armine Sandford
Producers:
Maurice Browne
John Crockett

Comus — Milton
All For Truth — Molière (trans. P. D. Cummins)
Great Catherine — G. B. Shaw
The Proposal — Anton Tchekov
(*The Last Enemy, The Proposal, Box and Cox,*
A Phoenix Too Frequent in Repertoire)

Joyce Allan
Maurice Daniels
Pamela Goodwin
Martin Heller
Hedley Lunn
John Ringham
Armine Sandford
Producer:
John Crockett
Dances:
Anne Stern

Dr Faustus — Marlowe
*Man Overboard — John Crockett
*Times Fool — Hans Holberg
(*Great Catherine, The Proposal, All For Truth,
A Phoenix Too Frequent*, in Repertoire)

Joyce Allan
Maurice Daniels
Pamela Goodwin
Collin Hansen
Martin Heller
Hedley Lunn
Raymond Parkes
John Ringham
Armine Sandford
Producers:
John Crockett
John Headley

1951 - 1952

*Strange Return — P. D. Cummins
(*Time's Fool* in Repertoire)

Maurice Daniels
Sybil Ewbank
Mona Glyn
Martin Heller
Anthony Hipwell
John Hoskin
John Ringham
Armine Sandford
Producer:
John Crockett

Tours Managers for The Compass Players were:

Mike Pelham
Brian Stapleton
Josephine Jemmett
Catherine Dunoon
Gerard Heller

APPENDIX B

A TYPICAL ITINERARY

ITINERARY — MARCH, 1951

Repertoire:

"Doctor Faustus" by Christopher Marlowe	— (F)
"Man Overboard" by John Crockett	— (MO)
"Jonah" by John Crockett	— (J)
"Great Catherine" with "Village Wooing" by Bernard Shaw	— (GC/VW)
"The Proposal" by Anton Tchekov with "A Phoenix Too Frequent" by Christopher Fry	— (P/PTF)
"All for Truth" by Moliere	— (AT)

Date.	Time.	Play.	Place of Performance.	Organiser.
1/3/51.	) 10. a.m.) 2. p.m.	J J	Condor Secondary Modern School.	) W. H. John Esq.,) Secondary Modern) School, Codnor, Derbys.
2/3/51.	) 2.30 p.m.) 6.30 p.m.	J J	Long Eaton Grange Secondary Modern School.	) F. W. Graham, Esq.,) The Grange Secondary) Modern School, Long) Eaton, Nottingham.) Long Eaton 543.
3/3/51.	7.15 p.m.	AT	The Modern School, Eccleshall.	) W. Hanscombe, Esq.,) Wincote, Eccleshall,) Staffs. Eccleshall 237.
4/3/51.		(Travelling)		
5/3/51.	7.30 p.m.	F	Padgate Training College.	) Miss D. Peach,) Padgate Training) College, Fearnhead,) Warrington, Lancs.) Warrington 2671/2.
6/3/51.		(Travelling)		
7/3/51.	7.15 p.m.	F	Ampleforth College, York.	) The Rev. E. O. Vanheems,) Ampleforth College,) York. Ampleforth 225.) Telegram "Vanheems,) Ampleforth College".
8/3/51.	2.15 p.m.	C	The Bar Convent Grammar School, York.	) Mother M. Thomas, IBVM.,) Bar Convent Grammar) School, York. York 3537.

161

INDEX

Page numbers given in italic type indicate illustrations and their captions

167

ERRATA

Page 3, line 42 — Edmund Rubbra
Page 9, line 36 — Monro
Page 90, line 2 — Thorndike
Page 125, line 43 — Ikon Theatre Company
Page 129, line 31 — position
Page 145, line 7 — whole

Page 136 line 22 - John Ridley